T0041523

Amazing Surfing Stories

Amazing Surfing Stories

Alex Wade

Reprinted by Fernhurst Books Limited in 2021
The Windmill, Mill Lane, Harbury, Leamington Spa, Warwickshire. CV33 9HP, UK
Tel: +44 (0) 1926 337488 | www.fernhurstbooks.com

Copyright © 2012 Alex Wade
The rights of Alex Wade to be identified as author of this work has been asserted in accordance with the UK Copyright, Designs and Patents Act 1988.

First published in 2012 by John Wiley & Sons Ltd

All rights reserved. No part of this publication may be reproduced, stored in a retrieval system or transmitted, in any form or by any means, electronic, mechanical, photocopying, recording, scanning or otherwise, except under the terms of the Copyright, Designs and Patents Act 1988 or under the terms of a licence issued by The Copyright Licensing Agency Ltd, Saffron House, 6-10 Kirby Street, London EC1N 8TS, UK, without the permission in writing of the Publisher.

Designations used by companies to distinguish their products are often claimed as trademarks. All brand names and product names used in this book are trade names, service marks, trademarks or registered trademarks of their respective owners. The Publisher is not associated with any product or vendor mentioned in this book.

This publication is designed to provide accurate and authoritative information in regard to the subject matter covered. It is sold on the understanding that the Publisher is not engaged in rendering professional services. If professional advice or other expert assistance is required, the services of a competent professional should be sought. The Publisher accepts no responsibility for any errors or omissions, or for any accidents or mishaps which may arise from the use of this publication.

A catalogue record for this book is available from the British Library
ISBN 978-1-119-94254-2

Cover photo © Sean Davey

Set in 12/14pt Garamond by Aptara Inc., New Delhi, India
Printed in Malta by Melita Press

This book is dedicated to my surfing sons, Harry and Elliot, and to the man in the east, Neil Watson

CONTENTS

Preface xi

Part One Going to Extremes

Child's Play? Definitely Not 3
Hold Down 7
Surviving the Atom Blaster 12
Oh My God (Take 1) 18
Size Matters 23

Part Two Tragic Tales

In Memory of Andy Irons 31
Veitch: RIP 36
QED 40
The Peterson Problem 44

Part Three When the Big Stuff Bites

A Bite out of Burle 51
People in Car Crashes Don't Stop Driving 55
Bare Hands and Bombs 59
The White Zone 66

CONTENTS

Part Four Gonzo Interlude

Being Dave Rastovich 75
A Thrust Too Far 87
Do You Know Russell Winter? 92
Four Surfers and a Painting 98

Part Five Contests and Communities

Higher than a High Five 105
Black Clouds and Bellyboards 109
Bad Boy Bobby and the New York Quiksilver Pro 114
The Big M 120
Lord Thurso, Cool in Caithness 123
A Debt at Dungeons 126
After *Rio Breaks* 133

Part Six Worldwide Waves

Seven Ghosts 139
Hokkaido – The Rights of Passage 145
1,300 Miles for a Wave 150
Ed's Left, aka the Spot with No Name 153
Loco on Lobos 157
The Lady in the Emerald Green Bathing Dress 162
Purring thanks to 'Da Cat' 168

Part Seven Obsession

Peg Leg Rik 175
Soldiers Get Stoked 179
The Daily Wavester 182
The Amazing Mr Slater 186

Part Eight Inspiration

Stoked 193
Colonel 'Mad Jack' Churchill 195

OMG (Take 2) 199
Dr Sarah and the Meaning of Surfing 204

Acknowledgements 208

PREFACE

This book aims to do what it says on the tin: it is a collection of amazing surfing stories. What, though, is an 'amazing' surfing story?

In many cases, the stories are demonstrably 'amazing', as in the tale of Laird Hamilton's infamous 'Millennium Wave' at Teahupoo on 17 August 2000, when he took surfing to a new level, or in two pieces which feature another Hawaiian hellman, Garrett McNamara. 'GMAC', as he is known, surfed what was subsequently ratified as a world record wave at Nazaré, off the coast of Portugal, in November 2011 (it came in at a hefty 78ft and is recounted in *Size Matters*), but perhaps even more astonishingly he has also surfed waves created by a calving glacier face. He described this outlandish Alaskan experience as being "like sitting underneath the Empire State Building, waiting for it to come down on you" (see *Child's Play*).

Hamilton and McNamara join other exponents of extreme surfing featured in this book, who include Shane Dorian (see *Hold Down*), Carlos Burle and Mark Visser. These men are well-known in the surfing community, and elsewhere – Australian surfer Visser especially is making a name for himself beyond surfing, thanks to achievements like surfing the legendary Maui break of Jaws at night (see *Surviving the Atom Blaster*). Other surfers and their stories may not be so embedded in the mass wave-riding consciousness, but are just as mind-boggling:

witness English surfer Andrew Cotton's fearlessness in *The White Zone*, and unsung, underground hero Tony Butt's commitment to big wave surfing in *Bare Hands and Bombs*.

The quality of amazement may not arise from a single act of derring-do. It may be down to the way a life was lived, and the way it ended, as in the stories of part two *Tragic Tales*. Or it might flow from the spirit of a competition (see *Higher Than a High Five*) – or its aftermath (*Bad Boy Bobby and the New York Quiksilver Pro*). Travel opens the mind and if it might not engender jaw-dropping as profound as a shark attack (see Bethany Hamilton's tale in *People in Car Crashes Don't Stop Driving*), a Rip Curl search in Sumatra led to some extraordinary moments in *Seven Ghosts*, while a South African surf trip by a Cornish photographer yielded two opposing sides of surf travel: on the one hand, words to treasure from surfing legend Miki Dora; on the other, the tragedy of a shark attack which ended in death.

Elsewhere, there are gentler stories that can legitimately wear the amazing tag. Did Agatha Christie really go on a surf trip when she famously disappeared for 11 days in December 1926? Read *The Lady in the Emerald Green Bathing Dress* to decide. There's an act of selflessness in a competitive world in *A Debt at Dungeons*, an obsessive nature to beat all others in *The Daily Wavester*, and wonderful examples of determination to surf despite adversity in *Peg Leg Rik* and *Soldiers Get Stoked*.

There's a mild Gonzo interlude, too. For me, Dave Rastovich's life is, quite simply, amazing – take a look at *Being Dave Rastovich* to disappear, for a while, into his world. Other less than conventional surf stories appear in this part (called, funnily enough, *Gonzo Interlude*) which is intended to create portraits rather than precision, rather like Tony Plant's painting of the last tree on earth, one viewed by Rasta, Dorian and Buttons Kaluhiokalani, among others, in *Four Surfers and a Painting*.

The stories end with inspirational tales. Colonel 'Mad Jack' Churchill was the first man to ride the Severn Bore – what a man he was, too. If ever there was one, Mad Jack's was a life well lived, as is Mark Cunningham's, the mesmerizingly good Oahu bodysurfer – see *OMG* (*Take 2*). Cunningham bodysurfs with the beauty of a dolphin; my own experience of surfing with them is recounted in *Stoked*.

Finally, the book's last story perhaps goes to show that this is a book of amazing surfing stories which does what it says on the tin – with a caveat. For me, one of my most amazing surfing experiences came not thanks to a monster 30ft wave, or a near death experience, or a barrel to beat all barrels or the slickest, most radical off-the-lip ever performed – still less by witnessing wave-riding genius or talking to any of the leviathans of the surf world – but through surfing waist-to-shoulder high waves on a balmy summer's eve at a local secret spot, in the company of a person I barely know. The break should have been crowded, as it always is in the summer, but unaccountably there was barely anyone around. Dr Sarah and I shared benign and mellow waves whose memory will last us a lifetime – that, for me, is the most amazing thing about surfing.

PART ONE

Going to Extremes

CHILD'S PLAY? DEFINITELY NOT

Garrett McNamara and Keali'i Mamala are not the first surfers to ride Alaskan waves. But they are the first, and possibly the last, to ride Alaskan waves which were generated by a calving glacier.

Midway through the trailer for George Casey's 1998 film *Alaska: Spirit of the Wild*, the camera pans over the deep crevasses of a glacier in a sequence filmed from a helicopter or a small plane. The landscape is frigid, stark and monumental, beautiful and yet inimical to man. Next is a head-on shot, probably from land, of the face of the glacier. A vast slab of ice detaches itself from the face and plummets into the water below. A huge and murky, mud-brown wave erupts, staggering in its velocity, only for the footage to move almost as quickly as the rhapsodic score and sweep from mountains to whales and other Alaskan wildlife. The trailer closes with an image of a grizzly bear cub playfully eating a fish.

Anyone who loves the great outdoors would feel stirred by the trailer, let alone the 40-minute Charlton Heston-narrated film. But if you happened to be a surfer, and you witnessed the waves created by the ice as it fell from the face of the glacier, what would you think? Would you think 'Wouldn't it be great to ride one of those waves?' Or would you conclude that any such enterprise would be the height of madness?

For Ryan Casey, who worked on *Spirit of the Wild* as the stills photographer, the sight of the glacier-generated waves wouldn't go away. A fanatical surfer, Casey believed that the waves were rideable. While working on the film in 1995 he had seen them peeling for 200 yards, and at serious size: the biggest offered faces of between 20 and 30 ft. The fact that the slabs of ice were falling onto an ice shelf which was a mere 18 inches in depth meant that these waves also had an awful lot of power, even forming barrels sometimes.

The scene of the phenomenon seen by Casey and those who worked on *Spirit of the Wild* was Child's Glacier, some 50 miles from the small city of Cordova in south-central Alaska. Between May and September, as the glacier inches forward, it 'calves' – chunks of ice collapse into the water of Copper River below, as the river undermines its face. Each year, the calving process draws the more intrepid kind of tourist. Intrepid because this is an elemental place, much visited by bears, especially when outsize calving occurs; the waves caused by the falling ice detonate like a round of artillery fire and can throw up salmon on the shore of the opposite river bank, some 300 yards away. Bears – and eagles – know the sound, and they will not spurn such an easy meal.

For a long time, Casey thought about the waves he'd seen at Child's Glacier. And then, one day, he mentioned them to a good friend. That man, Oahu-based Garrett McNamara, was the kind to say 'Let's do it'. In 2007, 12 years after Casey worked on *Spirit of the Wild,* he and McNamara, along with a formidable Hawaiian surfer by the name of Keali'i Mamala, ventured to Alaska to do what no man had ever done before, and what very few, if any, will ever do again. They set up camp opposite Child's Glacier for a week and took on the waves created by ice falling from a 300 ft high glacier face.

"It was intense," says McNamara, whose frame and features look as if they have been hewn from rock. With deep, dark eyes and his black hair cut in a boxer's crewcut – there are neither the blue eyes nor the long, flowing blonde locks of surf cliché here – McNamara, or 'GMAC' as he is known, is one of surfing's characters. There is something primeval about him, something immutable. He brings an intensity to the mere uttering of the word 'intense', let alone in the way he lives his life.

Despite hailing from inland Massachusetts, GMAC has blazed a remarkable trail in surfing, which includes victory in the tow surfing world cup and a prodigious session at Praia de Norte, Nazaré, in Portugal 2011, when he rode what was widely cited as a world record 90 ft wave. McNamara has also earned a reputation as one of the best Teahupoo surfers. He has pushed the limits of stand up paddle board (SUP) surfing, taking SUPs deep into barrels at places like Jaws. But as much as the undoubted prowess required for such exploits, McNamara is known for his fearlessness. He looks like a gladiator and, by all accounts, acts like one too. If anyone could feel sanguine about sitting for hours underneath a towering glacier face, waiting for house-sized seracs of ice to cascade into icy river water, it is surely him.

McNamara's trip to Child's Glacier was the first time he had visited Alaska. "We were there for 10 days," he says. "We spent seven of them in the water waiting for blocks of ice to fall. It was daylight for 20 hours, which made for long, full-on and very cold days. The water was freezing." At 34 degrees Fahrenheit – which equates to around one degree Celsius – this statement is nigh on exact. McNamara and Mamala were suitably kitted out in thick wetsuits with 7 mm gloves and booties, not to mention a 2 mm survival suit complete with a helmet. They took a support crew and two jetskis: there was no way that it would be possible to paddle in to the glacier's waves. Moreover, jetskis would also enable them to outrun waves if need be.

And so it proved. "The first day was terrifying," says McNamara. "It was like sitting underneath the Empire State Building, waiting for it to come down on you." So frightening was the pair's first day that they were tempted to give up and return to Hawaii. "We thought about it. We had a feeling that maybe we'd taken on more than we could handle. We couldn't predict exactly where the ice would sheer off and fall, and on the first day it seemed like the whole glacier was dropping into the river. On top of that the place was eerie; we were miles from anywhere, co-existing with brown and black bears and a bunch of salmon. The whole atmosphere made you feel small and scared, and then the sound of the ice when it smashed into the river – it was awesome, really, really heavy. But we decided to stay and try again."

Their perseverance paid off. As the days passed, McNamara and Mamala fell into a routine, heading out on their jetski across the river to the gargantuan wall of the glacier and then taking turns to make passes underneath it. By doing so the surfer driving the jetski would be able to turn and tow the other into the path of an oncoming wave, hopefully picking it up as it peeled to the left or right once the debris of shards of ice had passed. They ended up catching waves every day for the remainder of the trip, some with faces at least double overhead high. Of standout rides, Mamala had a left that seemed to go on forever; McNamara had what he calls "a little shampoo job" on a right-hander. Tourists and fishermen who had ventured as far as the viewing point on the riverbank opposite were treated to an extraordinary spectacle: never could they have expected to make the trek to Child's Glacier and witness two surfers going about their business.

A summer's week at play underneath the terminus of Child's Glacier was enough. It was time to go home. By this point, McNamara had become convinced that calving glaciers are capable of producing the biggest waves in the world: "They could definitely produce bigger waves. It depends on how big the glacier is, how much water it displaces and how deep the water is and if there is a bottleneck where the swell hits. You could possibly find the biggest waves in the world like Lituya Bay."

A family man – he has three children (Ariana, Titus and Tiari) with Nicole, whom he says is "the love of my life" – McNamara is comfortable with risk. "I've been doing this kind of thing all my life so it's just how it has always been." He's also at ease about the model he provides for his children: "I encourage my kids to follow their own dreams and do what they're passionate about." But he describes his experiences at Child's Glacier as "the most horrifying, closest to death, heaviest rush I have ever experienced." Amazingly, he also says "I can't really get a rush like that anymore in the ocean."

Even for a man of McNamara's capabilities, it seems that glacier surfing isn't child's play. Asked if he would ever do it again, McNamara is emphatic: "Never again. It was as extreme as it gets. Definitely not."

HOLD DOWN

A Two-Wave Beating at Maverick's Leads to Inspiration.

Shane Dorian knows what he's doing in big surf. In fact, as a member of surfing's 'new school', which came to prominence in the 1990s, he knows what he's doing in any kind of surf. The man, who is the son of a stunt double for Elvis Presley, is just as good at getting air and sliding on the lip as he is at paddling into massive Jaws and charging Teahupoo.

But however good you are, sometimes things go wrong. As Dorian puts it: "Todd Chesser, Donnie Solomon, Mark Foo, Sion Milosky – they were all super-fit, confident guys. They all died big wave surfing. It can happen to anyone." It nearly did to Dorian at Maverick's in February 2009.

Dorian had flown from his home on Hawaii's Big Island to the notorious northern California big wave break on 13 February – his wife Lisa's birthday. He recalls the motivation clearly: "I'd never surfed Maverick's but had been building up to it for years. The chart showed a huge swell so I went."

Lean and ultra-disciplined – he is in the gym every day for a two-hour session starting at 5 o'clock in the morning – Dorian speaks quietly, calmly, almost gently. But despite the provenance of its name, there's nothing gentle about Maverick's. Legend has it that the break acquired its name in honour of an exuberant, white-haired German Shepherd puppy called Maverick. Sometime in March 1958 three surfers, Alex Matienzo, Jim Thompson and Dick Notmeyer, paddled out to surf waves which they had seen breaking off Pillar Point, just north of Half Moon Bay. Maverick was with Matienzo, and, accustomed as he was to swimming in the sea (or perhaps mindful of his role as man's best friend), decided to take to the water too. The loyal canine was later tied to a car bumper for his own good, allowing Matienzo, Thompson and Notmeyer to surf overhead waves about a quarter of a mile from the shore. They were content to leave it at that, but named the break they'd pioneered Maverick's Point.

The wave remained unridden for nearly two decades, but in 1975 Jeff Clark, who grew up in Half Moon Bay, decided to take on the break which he recalled one of his high school teachers calling 'Maverick's'. Clark's name has since become synonymous with it, and no wonder. Aged 17, having watched Maverick's breaking on a number of occasions, Clark paddled out with the words of a school-friend ringing in his ears: his friend said he'd "call the Coast Guard and tell them where I last saw you". It was obvious that surfing Maverick's was going to be dangerous – the wave breaks a long way from the shore, it's cold and murky, prone to ferocious currents and sharky – but Clark was smitten. For 15 years, he surfed the wave alone, even learning to surf switchfoot so that he could ride frontside at Maverick's whether it was breaking to the left or to the right.

Eventually and inevitably, word got out. Surfers from northern California's surf city, Santa Cruz, began to drive the few miles north to Maverick's, inspired by tales of hollow and powerful 20 ft beasts which had been ridden by Dave Schmidt and Tom Powers, the first men to surf the wave with Clark. Next up came a southward influx, as San Francisco's big wave surfers learned of the break. Then, with the publication of a photograph in a 1990 issue of *Surfer* magazine, the surfing world knew all about Maverick's. Within a few years, its 'discovery' had metamorphosed into the stuff of legend thanks first to Santa Cruz surfer Jay Moriarty and then to Hawaiian big wave charger Mark Foo. Aged just 16, Moriarty took off late on a monster right-hander, only to freefall down the face into a wipeout of seismic magnitude; the incident was captured on film, and made the cover of *Surfer*. Four days after Moriarty's skirmish with death, Foo, who had flown over from Oahu with fellow big wave surfer Ken Bradshaw, died while surfing an 18 ft wave at Maverick's.

Foo's demise shocked the surfing world. Handsome, slick when it came to self-promotion, and yet deserving of the accolades that came his way thanks to his fearlessness and poise in giant surf, Foo coined one of surfing's great quotes: "If you want the ultimate thrill, you've got to be willing to pay the ultimate price." The media loved it; the media loved Foo; but soundbite turned into bitter reality on 23 December 1994 when Foo, surfing Maverick's for the first time, caught a rail and wiped out. Maverick's was so crowded that day that it wasn't until hours later, when his body was found floating on the surface, that people noticed his absence.

Shane Dorian knew Foo well. He also knew the next man to die at Maverick's, Hawaiian surfer Sion Milosky. Kauai born and raised, Milosky lost his life at Maverick's after a two-wave hold down on 16 March 2011. What happened was dramatically described by another Maverick's surfer, Ryan Seelbach: "On this particular wave, [Sion] was right in the heart of the bowl. He made the drop, got to the bottom, did a bottom turn and the thing just mowed him over. There was no making it to the shoulder on that." Although he was later plucked from the water by Nathan Fletcher – a top-rated surfer who once snapped his femur while surfing Pipeline (on a benign, 4-6 ft day) – and given CPR on the beach, there was nothing anyone could do to save Milosky. Videographer Chris Killen, who was involved in the attempt to save Milosky's life, distilled the essence of Maverick's thus: "They cut his suit off, and we found a flotation device in his suit and it freaks me out that a guy like Sion, arguably one of the gnarliest big wave surfers in the world, could not survive a Maverick's hold down, even with a floatation device. Once they put him in the ambulance, we knew he was gone."

Dorian's first Maverick's session seemed to augur well. As he recalls, "The first day was really good. It was really big but I felt comfortable and confident." But on day two, Maverick's took on a darker hue. "The next day was supposed to be smaller, but it wasn't. I fell on a wave and had a two-wave hold down."

Dorian speaks in an even, measured tone which masks the drama of that day. According to one witness, he was under water for over a minute. "I was thinking to myself 'Stay calm, stay calm, stay calm' but after a while it was impossible not to panic. I knew I was getting close to blacking out. I had to start fighting and scrambling for the surface. It was either that or die. Just before I surfaced, I thought 'That's it, there's no chance, I'm not coming up'. I thought about Lisa, about my son Jackson and daughter Charlie. But I did. There was just time to catch a breath before the next wave hit me."

There was then yet another wave, pushing Dorian in towards the rocks before Frank Quirarte, a photographer known for his coverage of Maverick's, came to the rescue. "I think I would have been OK by that stage, but was glad to see Frank arrive on his jetski," says Dorian. There followed two days in which he felt "really out of it. I had concussion and my body felt battered. I slept for a whole day and night and had a headache for two days. I was so spaced out that I forgot to ring Lisa and say Happy Birthday."

But as Dorian reflected on his experience at Maverick's on the plane back to Hawaii, inspiration struck. The idea for what he subsequently christened 'the V1-Suit' crystallised. "I'd been experimenting with foam floatation in wetsuits but realised that these wouldn't be enough at a place like Maverick's. The idea of a wetsuit with an inflatable air bladder came to me and as soon as I was home I went online to see if there was anything like it. I was really surprised but there wasn't. I did some more research and then got in touch with Hub Hubbard, Billabong's wetsuit designer. It took another five or six months but then one day a package arrived in the mail. It was the first prototype of the suit, using a CO_2 cartridge to inflate the bladder when it's pulled by a ripcord. I tested it the same day in calm water and couldn't believe how quickly it brought me to the surface."

Dorian and Hubbard went on to develop the V1 (which stands for 'vertical ascent') suit with maritime safety product manufacturer Mustang Survival, but testing it in calm water would only ever provide a rudimentary indication of whether it would work. The acid test would come in big waves, and soon enough an opportunity came in the form of a Cortes Bank paddle-in session. Dorian had already worn the suit at Maverick's but hadn't needed to use it; no surprise that he says "I wasn't about to fall there on purpose, just to test it." His chance came at Cortes Bank, another leviathan in the pantheon of world-class big waves. The bank is a 25-mile-long island lying just below the surface of the water (its highest underwater peak, Bishop Rock, sometimes sits as little as three feet below the surface), some 100 miles west of San Diego. There, before mist swept in to make surfing impossible, Dorian "had a bad wipeout. I got pounded and pushed down really far and knew that this was the time to test the suit. As soon as I pulled the ripcord I stopped panicking, because it brought me to the surface so quickly. I didn't even swim, I just let the thing take me up. I couldn't believe how well it worked."

Dorian has since tested the suit on a number of other occasions, and reckons he hasn't been held under for more than 10 seconds whenever he's used it. Word about the V1-Suit soon spread, so too did demand for it, among the big wave community at least. "I designed the suit to save lives," says Dorian. "It's not for the mass market. Initially I had a list of 10 guys who might want one but the list just keeps growing. Mark Healey and Kelly Slater both have the suit, and people keep emailing me about it."

On the back of the V1-Suit there is a disclaimer of liability. Shane Dorian knows better than anyone that when it comes to big wave surfing, you might be able to do things to lessen the risk, but you'll never eliminate it completely – least of all, it seems, at a break like Maverick's.

SURVIVING THE ATOM BLASTER

When Australian professional surfer Mark Visser decided to try and ride Jaws by night, he had no idea quite how draining the experience would be.

"It vaporized me. I felt like my body went into little particles."

Laird Hamilton's summary of what a wipeout at Jaws feels like is all the more apposite given the name first coined for Maui's legendary reef break. "Before it was 'Jaws'," says Gerry Lopez, aka 'Mr Pipeline', "we called it 'Atom Blaster' because it broke like an atomic bomb. It's a super freak wave."

Jaws entered the surf world's consciousness thanks to two events in 1994. First came that year's September issue of *Surfer* magazine, which featured the wave, although its precise location was not given, and then a few weeks later, came *Endless Summer II.* Bruce Brown's update of his seminal 1964 celebration of surfing showed Jaws breaking at size, and emerged as the most memorable sequence in the film. It put Peahi (its Hawaiian name, meaning 'beckon') on the map, although the wave had been ridden since the late 80s and early 90s by hard-charging windsurfers such as Dave Kalama, Rush Randle and Mike Waltz. The mid-90s saw the advent of tow-in surfing; by the end of the decade Jaws – which only breaks over 20 ft around six times a year – was as well-known as Waimea Bay (and, when it worked, probably more crowded).

Since the early 90s to the present day, Hamilton has been the surfer who is most regularly associated with Jaws. To a degree, this is down to his exceptional media savvy: if there is one surfer who knows how to talk amiably to journalists, it is the 6 ft 3 inch, 220-pound, blond, square-jawed and muscular Hamilton, who was born at San Francisco university in an experimental salt-water sphere. Mostly though, Hamilton's dominance of the line-up at Jaws is simply because he is its best surfer. Time and again he has proved this by challenging the wave rather than merely riding it, carving turns on its vast, open faces and slipping into barrels as if Jaws was an 8 ft walk in the park rather than the terrifying 80 ft beast that it can be.

But for all that Hamilton is Peahi's virtuoso performer, there is one thing that even he has never done. It is something that only one man has done. It is something that very few people, if any, will ever do – and that fewer still would even conceive of doing. Anyone for surfing a pumping, fully awoken, bone-gnawing Jaws by night?

The man who can lay claim to this feat is Australian surfer Mark Visser – and his achievement began with a friend's dream.

"A friend called Christo had a dream about riding big waves at night," says Visser, an ultra-fit 29-year-old dubbed the 'Lung Fish' on account of his ability to hold his breath under water for over six minutes. "His dad owned a torch company, and it got him thinking about whether it would be possible to ride big waves at night if they were lit up. He had this weird dream of me surfing while wearing a miner's light. It was one of those things that we talked about in the pub."

If the genesis was unusual, the planning was precise – and again involved a close friend. "My best mate, Ryan Stewart, pushed me to think of a way of realising Christo's dream. Ryan was always on at me, making me think it through, and I began working with submarine lighting engineers to develop the illumination necessary to complete the project. Initially, it failed time and time again, but finally, after three years, we developed a mechanism to make the light reflect against the wave, thereby allowing the rescue crew to keep track of me. At the same time, I could see where I was going without being blinded by the light. All in all, four years after he had his dream Christo's idea came to fruition."

More to the point, it came to fruition at Jaws – one of the most dangerous waves on earth, as Visser knew all too well from personal experience. "Jaws is a gnarly place. The first time I surfed there I got washed into the cliff. I didn't forget the experience in a hurry and although I've surfed the place many times since, you can never take it for granted."

Visser's first session at Jaws gave him a visceral sense of the truth of renowned Hawaiian big wave surfer Darrick Doerner's much-quoted line: "When you go down [at Jaws], and you will, it will be the most devastating experience of your life." But Visser, who quit the World Qualifying Tour (WQS) because he grew weary of surfing small waves, thrives on danger. Although he avows that "I wouldn't consider myself a daredevil", Visser's post-WQS predilection for giant surf might, to many people, put him squarely in this category. He has surfed many of the world's most demanding waves, from Teahupoo in Tahiti, Cloudbreak in Fiji and Hawaii's best spots to Australian monsters such as Shipstern's Bluff, Cow Bombie in Western Australia and another fearsome WA wave known only as 'The Slab'. But aside from such high profile derring-do, Visser has also amassed an impressive series of big wave contest results, placing fifth in a 2006/2007 tow-in tour event in Chile, seventh in Oregon's Nelscott Reef Big Wave Paddle-In event, and runner up in the 2008/2009, 2009/2010 and 2010/2011 Oakley ASL Big Wave Awards. Visser, who began surfing at the age of 10 and went on to represent the Australian schoolboys team, has also had several waves entered into the XXL awards for biggest wave ridden.

"I really want to push myself on a whole range of different levels," says Visser, but in deciding to night-surf Jaws he got more than he bargained for, as much in the build-up, as on the night. "It was so draining in the lead-up to the night ride, everything was so intense and

I was so scared by what was looming that I didn't sleep properly," says the goofy-footer, whose home is on Australia's Sunshine Coast. "Every day for about a week I would wake up at 5am in a hot sweat. It was the most traumatic experience in the lead-up to anything I've ever done in my life."

There were logistical problems galore too, from the creation of custom-made LED lighting built into a buoyancy vest and on Visser's surfboard, to finding a jetski driver on the night. It took several modifications to get the lighting just right, so that it wouldn't hinder the vision of Visser, the jetski drivers and the helicopter pilots, but then the original jetski team dropped out. "We had teed up some drivers for the project," explains Visser, "but I think reality set in – they pulled out at the last minute, saying it was a suicide mission. Luckily, my regular tow-surfing partner, Yuri Soledade, lives on Maui and was happy to step in at the last minute. I've competed with Yuri in big wave events all around the world, so it was actually a relief that he was able to be in the water with me." Helicopters fitted with special lights to light up the sea in case Visser wiped out were used, but finding a pilot wasn't easy either: "It was really difficult getting helicopter pilots willing to be involved in the project as it was so dangerous," says Visser. "But we were going to do it one way or another and had an evacuation plan set up on the cliff if we needed it."

Months of preparation for the night-surf saw Visser work with safety teams, members of the special forces and a number of Australia's best fitness coaches, all of whom conditioned Visser to deal with the unexpected. "The training with the coaches was tough," he told journalist Cassandra Murnieks, who writes for *The Australian*. However, training did not simply consist of testing the technology in smaller waves at night in Australia and endless work-outs, it also included paddling in shark-infested seas for up to six hours. As Visser said to Murnieks, "The coaches pushed me and they had me paddling at night in shipping channels and in shark-infested waters. On one night, I was told to paddle in a shark area for six hours. For the first two hours, it was pitch-black and I kept coming into contact with fish and jellyfish, which freaked me out a bit. But after the first two hours, my eyes had adjusted to look out for the shadows and it became easier after that. If I had all of those things under control, it was one less thing to worry about when it actually came to surfing Jaws."

But the fear factor on the night was undiminished. Jaws was breaking in the 30-40 ft range; big enough by day in anyone's book, but an even scarier proposition in darkness. In the heaving ocean, and barely able to see, Visser's senses were even more finely tuned than usual. "In daylight, you can see and react to how the wave is bending and turning, whereas at night you can't control any of that and you're really in nature's hand. You have to use all your senses because you can't see. As much as is humanly possible, you have to be at one with the wave." And fear is part of the process: "I always feel fear, but I'm OK with it," says Visser. "I accept it and I deal with it as I go along."

Eventually, at 2am on Thursday 20 January 2011, Visser took to the water with just Soledade to tow him into waves and another man driving a rescue ski. Forty minutes passed before he caught his first wave; when it came, it didn't alleviate the fear. "I felt rattled," says Visser. "It was just so strange being out there in darkness. I was super scared about falling because I could have gone over the falls backwards. Because it was night I couldn't guarantee that the jetski would be able to see me if I was in trouble. But after my second wave I started to feel more confident. I began to read the waves and have a feel for how they would break."

Visser ultimately spent three and a half hours night-surfing Jaws, by the end of which he had ridden 12 waves. He wiped out on the last one – "when the choppers turned their lights on for fun. They had no idea it was totally blinding me" – but lived to tell the tale, one which owes its inspiration not merely to a friend's dream but to two of Visser's heroes. "Muhammad Ali and Michael Jordan have been hugely influential in my life," he says. "They both achieved things despite adversity, despite people telling them they couldn't do what they set out to do."

Since the exploit Visser has acquired another nickname. He is not just the Lung Fish but also the 'Night Rider', and what's more, the man who says he's not a daredevil would night-surf Jaws again.

"I would do it again, yes, but I wouldn't want a camera crew there next time. I'd rather just go out in waves that I know and surf alone, soaking the whole thing up with no pressure."

Meanwhile, the Night Rider has another project – parachuting into the open ocean in search of 100 ft waves. The idea seems mad, its execution impossible, but if there's one man who can do it, it's Mark Visser, though even he admits that 'Operation Deep Blue' has a limit. "Airdropping into the sea, thousands of miles from land, in search of rogue 100 ft waves is not something I'd do at night."

OH MY GOD (TAKE 1)

On 17 August 2000 Laird Hamilton changed the face of surfing.

"Surfing's not about conquering the ocean. You're given an allowance and you survive moments. When you surf a wave well, you're maximising the ocean's allowance – that's all."

So says Laird Hamilton, whose oceanic exploits have seen him described by many among the surfing cognoscenti as the best big wave surfer yet to walk the earth. Inevitably, there are naysayers who say that Laird's good, but that ultimately he's just one of an elite coterie of big wave hellmen, all of whom regularly defy physics and the limits of what is believed to be humanly possible. The doubters argue that if Laird has an edge, it's in being that much better at self-promotion, at getting his image out to a waiting and all too eager public. They say that as much as his instincts in the water are preternatural, the way in which there's always a camera lens on hand or a TV crew nearby, ready to catalogue his every mind-warping ride, is just as uncanny.

Anyone in this camp needs only to think of one of Laird's rides to revise their view. That wave – dubbed 'the Millennium Wave' – was ridden on 17 August 2000 at the Tahitian reef break of Teahupoo.

Teahupoo – which translates to 'Place of Skulls' – had been surfed before. As with many of the world's most dangerous waves, bodyboarders had blazed a trail. Mike Stewart, a man the same age as Hamilton, who grew up on Hawaii's Big Island, rode the absurd, outsize, cartoonish barrels of Teahupoo in 1986. He returned often to freefall into the trough of the wave, race its pulsating lip and somehow navigate his way, inches above razor-sharp coral, to the safety of the channel. Stewart's tales of Teahupoo did much to put it on the map, not least because they were relayed to the late Sean Collins, the founder of the hugely influential surf forecasting website Surfline.com. When Collins saw the photographic evidence, and a little later when he visited Teahupoo himself, he had no doubt that this wave was "the heaviest wave in the world".

The word was out, and pro surfers started making their way to Teahupoo, initially calling the wave they discovered 'The End of the Road'. The name came because the paved road literally ended at the town of Teahupoo, but, as the wave came to be ridden, its capacity to mark the end of the road for those surfing it also became literal: since 2000, five surfers have died at Teahupoo. They include local Tahitian surfer Briece Taerea, who was killed at Teahupoo in April 2000, just a few months before Hamilton's extraordinary ride. Taerea tried to duck-dive a wave with a 25 ft face but was thrown over the falls and smashed head first onto the reef. He sustained two broken neck bones and a broken spine, and was paralyzed from the neck down. Despite being recovered from the water, he died two days later.

The consequences of getting it wrong at Teahupoo didn't deter surfing companies from holding events there. First was Gotcha, whose inaugural World Championship Tour event at Teahupoo in 1999, was won by Australian surfer, and later world champion, Mark Occhilupo. Since 2001, Billabong has held the Billabong Pro Teahupoo each year, an event which has been won by luminaries of surfing including Kelly Slater, the late Andy Irons and Bobby Martinez. Along the way, the wave which was reputedly first surfed by Tahitian Thierry Vernaudon (in 1985, but not at significant size) has scared away any number of would-be contenders, and no wonder. As Sean Collins said, once it reaches 12-15 feet (with faces therefore between 25-40 feet) Teahupoo mutates and becomes "a monster".

At this size, paddling in to Teahupoo is not possible. The combination of geology, swell size and direction and physics means that what seems to be a small wave from the rear is relentlessly sucking water towards its face and then depositing all its energy onto the reef, so that the wave breaks below sea level. At this size, Teahupoo is simply too fast and vertical to be safely paddled into, and a fall is to run a serious risk of death or severe injury.

Hence, when Laird Hamilton tackled Teahupoo, he was towed in by Darrick Doerner, himself an exceptional surfer and waterman (and the stunt double for Patrick Swayze in Kathryn Bigelow's 1991 surf-heist movie *Point Break*). 'Double D', as Doerner is known, actually urged Hamilton *not* to let go of the tow rope. Hamilton recalls hearing him shouting "Don't let go!", and reckons other voices – those watching from the safety of the channel, on boats or other jetskis, or perhaps inside his head – were also screaming that discretion was the better part of valour. But Hamilton was always going to let go. His whole life was geared to riding a wave that surf writer Paul Holmes described as not "just a wave, more like a 20-foot shift in sea level, the entire mass of the South Pacific ocean surging onto an almost bone-dry reef – countless tons of water, immeasurable energy about to be unleashed".

Against a backdrop of benign sunshine and the alluring crystalline blue of the Pacific, Hamilton let go of the tow rope. Doerner sped away, steering his jetski over the crest of the wave which was about to implode and quite possibly destroy even the 220-pound, 6 ft 3 inch frame of Hamilton. Those watching gasped, stood, stared, caught their breath – and then whooped with amazement. This was a wave of diabolical proportions, one whose lip and face was so thick and unforgiving that a fall would have meant certain death. But somehow, Hamilton conceived of a low crouch with the hand of his trailing arm almost level with the outside rail of his board. No one had done this before; no one had reacted so precisely, so perfectly and so instinctually to counter the hydraulics of the wave. Hamilton's act – of faith, of conditioning, of sheer self-preservation – saw him spat out, alive and unscathed, to the astonishment of the surfing world.

Many of the resulting eulogies spoke of how Hamilton had 'conquered' Teahupoo (allied to which he is often said to have 'mastered' Jaws, the big wave break on Maui with which he is indelibly linked), but the man himself does not agree with such metaphors. "Surfing's not about conquering the ocean. You've been allowed to be on that wave. You need to keep this in mind and be careful not to set yourself up to get spanked. There's no discrimination in the sea, no referees, no time-out, no room for being 'too tired,' it's just you in the sea. You don't go round telling everyone about the big waves you've ridden, showing them posters – you let your actions speak louder than words."

Nor was Hamilton insouciant about that ride of 17 August 2000, which featured on the cover of *Surfer* magazine with a simple strapline: "Oh my god . . . ". "I felt fear at Chopes [Teahupoo's nickname], for sure. I had an inner battle going on there. I took a couple of waves before that one [on the *Surfer* cover] and the inner struggle was mounting. I was saying each time, 'jump,' 'don't jump,' 'jump'. That kind of inner turmoil is normal in a situation when you feel your life is vulnerable; the argument went on, but on that wave time seemed to slow down. It was an extremely emotional situation, a dream come true. You've been gearing your life for this moment and suddenly you get the chance to experience it. That wave broke the barrier, it made it easier to do other things afterwards. It was like breaking the sound barrier or the four-minute mile."

Hamilton reckons his pursuit of riding big waves has resulted in over 1,000 stitches. "I've broken my left leg, broken my left ankle five times and separated my shoulder," he says. The scars and breaks have come at the same time as family commitments – he has been married twice and has three daughters – but he is at ease with taking risks which sometimes result in wipe-outs that he describes as "like stepping on a mine".

"Surfing is what I do. It's where I'm comfortable. I feel fear – you have to. It's part of the respect for the ocean that you have to have. If you're not fearful you're ignorant and blind. So I feel afraid, yes, but I also feel totally at home in the ocean. I want people to value me for who I am, and the ocean is who I am. I brought my kids into the world – they didn't ask to be born – but it seems to me to be wrong if I stop being myself because of them. Just living is a dangerous job. I get more afraid flying than surfing. The biggest sin in the world would be if I lost my love for the ocean."

A last word for the naysayers. If there is a man who has surfed a 100 ft wave, it's Hamilton. The session happened at a Maui break called Egypt. It saw Hamilton heroically save his then tow partner Brett Lickle, and was chronicled by Susan Casey in her book *The Wave.* But not a single photograph exists.

SIZE MATTERS

On 1 November 2011 Garrett McNamara rode the biggest wave yet surfed. Or did he?

The Massachusetts town of Pittsfield is not known for its surfers. This should not come as a surprise, for Pittsfield, once ranked as the 20th most secure place to live in the United States, is some 140 miles from the coast. If one were to search out the surf breaks either side of the coast from Boston, one would find that the sea temperature is freezing and the wave quality inconsistent. Anyone drawn to surfing, but brought up in Pittsfield, would have to be seriously dedicated to become anything better than average. Or move.

Fortunately for him, this is just what Garrett McNamara's parents did in 1978. Better yet, in eschewing the comforts of Pittsfield, they decided to opt for surfing paradise as their new home, settling on the north shore of Oahu a couple of years before Garrett became a teenager. Garrett and his younger brother Liam immediately gravitated to surfing, and became fixtures in line-ups at places like Pipeline, Rocky Point, Waimea and Sunset. Both acquired sponsorship deals, and were especially fêted in Japan.

In the early 1990s, Garrett set his sights on big wave surfing rather than contests. He resolved to do two things: one, to win the prestigious Eddie Aikau Invitational, an event held at Waimea Bay in honour of the legendary Hawaiian lifeguard Eddie Aikau, which only takes place when waves exceed 20 ft (as measured, Hawaiian-style, from the back); and two, to win the Tow Surfing World Cup at the Maui break of Jaws. He achieved the latter, and along the way, made a name for himself as a big wave hellman *nonpareil*, thanks to well-documented derring-do at places like Teahupoo, Jaws and Maverick's and by surfing waves generated by a calving glacier off the coast of Alaska in the summer of 2007. This rather peculiar enterprise entailed sitting beneath the edge of the glacier in frigid water, waiting for it to shed blocks of ice whose 300 ft fall into the sea would generate a surfable wave. Garrett was there, ready and waiting, with surfing partner Keali'i Mamala. The very idea, as much as its execution, suggested that the limits of what is feasible in extreme surfing had been pushed as far as they could go.

But then in 2010, came a trip to Nazaré's Praia do Norte (North Beach). Outsize surf was ridden; Nazaré lodged itself in Garrett's mind. If Portugal had long been on the radar of the surfing cognoscenti – both for its excellent year-round surf and big wave potential – what followed at the same spot, on 1 November 2011, arguably took extreme surfing to yet another level. That day, Garrett McNamara – or 'GMAC', as he is known – rode a 90 ft wave.

Or did he? As images of McNamara looking like anything but a citizen of Pittsfield were beamed around the world, the naysayers set to work. No, they said, GMAC's wave wasn't 90 ft. Sure, it was big, but it wasn't as big as the accepted world record for big wave surfing – Californian surfer Mike Parsons' 2008 ride at Cortes Bank, logged by the Guinness Book of Records as a 77 ft wave. Maybe it was 70 ft, or even 75 ft, but no, Parsons still had the record.

The naysayers had another reason to vent their ire. It seemed that McNamara had 'claimed' the world record. Surfing etiquette dictates that claims should only ever be made silently, to oneself and perhaps a trusted friend or loved one; they should be ratified either by official panels, if appropriate, or by word of mouth, as experts and gurus let it be known that say, Ken Bradshaw really did surf an 85 ft wave in Hawaii (another contender for 'biggest wave ever surfed'). But within days of a ride that was, by any criteria remarkable, it appeared that McNamara's publicity machine had gone into overdrive, with a press release doing the rounds headed "Garrett McNamara Breaks World Record Riding The Biggest Wave Ever In Nazaré!" Later, it transpired that the release was not of McNamara's making; he had neither written nor authorised it. What he had done, though, was send video footage of the wave to an oceanographer and a number of highly reputable surfers (including Kelly Slater and pioneer of big wave surfing Greg Noll). All apparently concurred that the wave could well have touched 90 ft. Or, as Slater tweeted: "I just saw a shot of Garrett Macnamara [sic] from Portugal on a stupidly big wave. He should post that thing ASAP. Looks like huge Jaws."

Nazaré itself was, until a short while ago, the quintessential Portuguese fishing village of yesteryear. Now, in a bid to snare the tourist Euro, it is undergoing a makeover, but its charm remains. Glimpses of the traditional costumes worn by fishermen and their wives can still be seen in Nazaré, while the even prettier village of Sitio on the headland above – reached by a funicular railway – is quieter, more elegant and typically Portuguese. None of this would have been in McNamara's mind on 1 November 2011, just as precisely calculating the size of the surf would come later, too. No, before entering the sea, McNamara would have been marvelling at the waves produced by a geological phenomenon known as the Nazaré canyon – a gap in the continental plate, extending eastwards out into the Atlantic, which is 3.1 miles deep and 106 miles long. And once in the sea, he would have been intent on two things, and two things only: riding massive surf – and surviving.

That day, one man was better placed than any other to assess the magnitude of McNamara's Nazaré wave – Al Mennie, an Irishman who is also known for his fearlessness in huge surf. Mennie regularly takes on the giant waves of the west coast of Ireland with Englishman Andrew Cotton ('Cotty', as he is known), and the pair had previously tow-surfed at Praia do Norte with McNamara in 2010. In previous sessions, the trio had been joined by Floridian surfer C.J. Macias, but on 1 November only McNamara, Mennie and Cotton were in the water.

"We had been in Nazaré for a couple of days," says Mennie, a tall, powerfully built man in his early thirties, "but the canyon hadn't really been doing it. But then, on 1 November, we woke up and it was on. We assessed the whole thing and decided we could safely attempt to ride what looked like the biggest Nazaré we had ridden yet. I had finally got my confidence back after a couple of wobbly days on a new tow board and I was amping to ride some huge waves. It was mind-blowing out there. The peaks were coming at us from every angle imaginable and at times we felt completely surrounded. On top of that, the swell direction was making the cliff area really dangerous with waves smashing 100 ft up the sandstone rock face with a massive, booming explosion. But we went for it. I surfed first, with Cotty towing me. We both rode the biggest waves of our lives – in the 60 ft range – before Cotty lost his board. The white water was so chaotic we decided against looking for it. Thankfully it washed up on the beach about 10 minutes later and didn't get smashed into the cliff."

Then it was GMAC's turn. Mennie recalls that he hadn't said much up to that point; indeed, that he hadn't seemed in tune with what was happening. This is very unlike the man, for as Mennie says, "Garrett always knows exactly what he wants. He's always 100 per cent focused on it. He wants to ride the biggest wave, and he channels all his energy into doing just that. On land, he's quiet but quite funny; in the water it's a different story. The first time we tow-surfed Nazaré together was classic. He was driving the jetski and rounded the headland before me. Straightaway he shouted at me to get ready. I didn't have the same visibility as him and shouted back that I wanted to check out what I'd be surfing first. GMAC just hollered 'What, are you fucking scared?' He's like a man possessed in the water."

Nicole, Garrett's partner, was watching the action unfold from the headland. With Cotton about to tow Garrett, Mennie heard Nicole "going nuts on the radio – 'Huge Set Approaching!', she screamed. I looked and could see a set of three waves on the horizon. I couldn't believe what I saw. They were mutants, at least 20 ft bigger than anything we'd surfed so far."

The trio have a system whereby the safety driver (in this case, Mennie) follows the other jetski and as soon as the surfer is on the wave, both skis go in one after another so that if the first ski misses the rescue the other is just seconds behind. This meant that when Cotton pulled Garrett into position, Mennie was following close behind, only to fade back. Before he did, he had a grandstand view of Garrett's wave. "Garrett was in the perfect spot right on the peak. I was sitting almost in front of the wave as Garrett started to make the perfect drop. He was going so fast on this giant wall of a lefthander. I was concerned he might fall with so much speed. As the wave passed me, both Cotty and I went after it to get him before the next wave could mow him down. The thing about surfing the canyon at Nazaré is that you have to take a high line to escape being avalanched by the white water; you can't drive off the bottom, as you can with other big waves. Fortunately that's what Garrett did. He got it just right."

And from Mennie's perspective, how big was Garrett's wave? "From where I was, I reckoned Garrett's wave was a solid 80 ft but I knew that from a more direct angle it would probably measure somewhere in the 90 ft range. History was made that day. It was an honour to be there with Garrett, and I don't see why he shouldn't be proud of what he achieved."

It is said that Nazaré acquired its name from a statue of the Virgin Mary brought from Nazareth by a monk in the fourth century. It is also said that on 1 November 2011 Garrett McNamara, formerly of Pittsfield, MA, rode the largest wave yet surfed, in the company of Al Mennie and Andrew Cotton. There are some who dispute this claim; there are many others who give credit where credit is due.

As for Nicole, Mennie recalls that shortly after Garrett's wave her voice was again heard on the radio, at the same time as a shoal of fish came to the surface next to the three surfers: "OK you guys, it's time to head back to the harbour." They were content to take her advice. As for Mennie, he believes that it is possible to ride a 120 ft wave at Nazaré. Meantime, GMAC's 1 November 2011 wave "is what it is. It's a bloody big wave."

Note: Garrett McNamara's Nazaré ride was later ratified by the Guinness Book of Records as the biggest wave yet surfed. It was officially classed as a 78 ft wave.

PART TWO

Tragic Tales

IN MEMORY OF ANDY IRONS

The best way to honour the legacy of one of surfing's greats might just be to confront the truth.

On 2 November 2010, three-times world surfing champion Andy Irons was found dead in a Dallas airport hotel room. He had checked in to the Grand Hyatt at 8.47am the previous morning, having flown to the US from Puerto Rico, where he had been too ill to compete in the Rip Curl Search event.

In Puerto Rico, Irons was seriously unwell. Doctors gave him an intravenous drip in his hotel room, and advised that he go to hospital. Irons refused. He signed a release form acknowledging that he had declined treatment and made arrangements to return home to the Hawaiian island of Kauai, where his wife Lyndie was expecting the couple's first child.

Irons never made it back to Kauai. He didn't get to see Lyndie again. He never saw his son, who was christened Andrew Axel by his mother.

In his attempt to return home to Kauai from Puerto Rico, Irons booked a flight to Miami on 31 October. He would then have to take another flight to Dallas/Fort Worth before he could travel to Hawaii. On Halloween night, Irons went partying in Miami. He made the 1 November 6.30am connecting flight to Dallas, but then checked in to the Grand Hyatt. Staff found him dead in bed the next day; they'd knocked on the door of his room and, gaining no response, had gone in to investigate.

No doubt such things happen from time to time in the lives of hotel employees, but whoever found Irons must have been in shock for some time, both because no one enters a hotel room expecting to find that its occupant has died and because Irons was so young – surely too young, at 32 and as a professional sportsman, to die.

The surf world was certainly shocked. Irons was one of the most famous surfers of all time, the face of surfing giant Billabong, a former world champion and regarded by many as the only surfer of the early 21st century who could have been better than Kelly Slater. If only he could have been more focused, or retained the winning mentality that saw him prevail on the ASP world tour three years in a row, in 2002, 2003 and 2004, or, whisper it as quietly as a six-inch wave gently caressing a shingle beach, not taken quite so many drugs.

Irons' death shocked the surf world, sure. But what was more shocking – that a brilliant athlete had a personality that meant he was likely to succumb to the temptations around him, or that the surf industry closed ranks, both before and after a favoured son's demise? For despite it being well-known that Irons enjoyed what is quaintly described as 'the party scene', and for all that the cognoscenti were well aware that, on Halloween night, he had been snorting cocaine (and was also apparently eager to get his hands on something stronger, perhaps crystal meth or heroin), the code of silence proved to be as dominant as the grief which followed Irons' death.

The Times asked me to write Irons' obituary. In the fact-checking process, I was advised in no uncertain terms not to make any reference to drugs, not, of course, by those commissioning me at the paper, but by well-placed sources in the surfing community. I played ball. The official line was that Irons had died of dengue fever. There was nothing by way of hard evidence to go on to rebut this, and to bolster my sense of not speaking ill of the dead, there was also the fact that Irons' wife was just weeks away from her due date. It seemed, then, both evidentially uncertain and insensitive to speculate that her husband had died from a drug overdose.

But in the weeks and months that followed, the wall of silence seemed to grow all the more impenetrable. Rumours swirled; none were confirmed; many were denied. Irons died of Lyme disease. Irons died of dengue fever. Irons died of stress. And then, what became the received orthodoxy: Irons died of a heart attack.

"Travelling while sick and suffering from an undiagnosed heart condition was more than even Andy could overcome," said a statement by the Irons family, while a tweet from Surfline.com said "Andy Irons died of sudden cardiac arrest due to a blocked artery. His heart was full of passion for life and surfing."

For many months, the truth was elusive. What remained clear were Irons' achievements. He was a three-time world champion and the four-time winner of the prestigious Hawaiian Triple Crown. As much as he excelled in competitive surfing, he was also fearless and talented in big waves. He took the aerial moves pioneered by Martin Potter, the 1989 World Champion, to a new level, startling onlookers with smoothly executed above-the-lip tricks that seemed to owe as much to skateboarding as surfing. Irons' all-round capabilities put him unquestionably in surfing's roll-call of greats. No wonder his prodigious talent led to what was dubbed 'the Irons Age' of surfing.

Irons, born in 1978 in Lihue on Kauai, had surfing in his blood. His father, Phil, was a surfer and his uncle Rick was the 1964 United States Invitational winner. Younger brother Bruce is also a professional surfer and his cousin, Ricky Irons Jr, is the publisher of California-based *Surfer* magazine. The heady blend of being brought up next to some of the best surf on the planet, having a younger brother who was also a superb surfer and hailing from a surfing family meant that competitive success came easily to Irons as a teenager. He won the Juniors' Division of the 1996 US Championships and also prevailed in both the junior and men's divisions of the National Scholastic Surfing Association championships. Later the same year, in 20 ft plus surf and against seasoned professional surfers, Irons won the HIC Pipeline Pro competition on Oahu.

He was still at school then, but the lure of a career as a professional surfer was irresistible. In 1997, Irons qualified for the ASP World Tour, going on to win the Tahiti Pro at Teahupoo. Over the next few years he propelled himself to ever greater heights, but it seems that demons accompanied him each step of the way.

"I don't think I missed a single party those first couple of years," said Irons, who eventually checked into Promises, a rehab facility for the rich and famous in Malibu, a decade later. He didn't stay for long that first time – just 10 days or so – but was there again for a second time the same year in November 2007. There were then rumours that Irons was going to give a tell-all confessional interview to a leading surfing magazine, but it never happened; instead, at the beginning of the 2009 season, he took a year off to avoid burn-out.

"I surf because . . . it keeps my life at an even keel. Without it I would tip into oblivion." Thus spoke the lean and solid, six foot tall Irons, echoing various comments made anonymously by a study group of big wave surfers to university academics Sarah Partington, Elizabeth Partington and Steve Olivier for their paper for *The Sport Psychologist* entitled *The Dark Side of Flow: A Qualitative Study of Dependence in Big Wave Surfing*. It seems that flow – which the authors describe as "an optimal state underpinning peak performance" – may be sought after but that it is not without its problems. Said one surfer: "There is a risk of dying, of breaking bones, but the feeling you get off it [flow] is like no other feeling in the world. The best drugs cannot get you the same level of ecstasy, [the] feeling of really good adrenaline. Once you get familiar with that feeling it's an addiction." For another: "The pleasure outweighs the risk . . . and maybe that's not saying much for my regard for my life, for my health, but I guess I am willing to take the chance . . . of any pain or suffering it might cause over the benefits of the rush."

Still another – Participant H – revealed that "You just get a taste for it and I think it becomes addictive almost. It's something you can't quench, you can't satisfy it and you chase it . . . it's there for a period of time and then you kinda hang your guns up for a while, dry out and then think when can I do it again? There is psychologically after all that is done, there is a depression almost. You are sort of depleted and the only way to satisfy it is to do it again. The addiction is kinda funny."

But Irons' addictive nature wasn't funny. His successive world titles, between 2002 and 2004, may have coaxed the ultra-competitive Kelly Slater out of retirement but by the time 2010 dawned the close-knit world of surfing knew all too well that his 2009 sabbatical hadn't worked. Irons continued to test his body to its limit and then, in November, came the end.

Cometh the end, cometh the cover-up, albeit, to take a charitable view, that it was a well-meaning one, a whitewash that wanted only to believe in Andy Irons, to keep his myth alive.

Seven months after Irons' death, on 10 June 2011, a report was released by Tarrant County medical examiner, Nizam Peerwani, which stated beyond doubt that there was evidence of cocaine, methamphetamine, methadone, a generic form of the anti-anxiety drug Xanax, and marijuana in Irons' system. Yes, said Peerwani's toxicology report, 'the primary and the underlying cause of death is ischemic heart disease', but yes too, 'Drugs, particularly methadone and cocaine, [were] other significant factors contributing to death.' A subsequent review of Peerwani's report by Bruce Goldberger, director of toxicology at Florida University's College of Medicine, argued that the high levels of Xanax and Methadone alone could have been fatal.

Notwithstanding the report, there are many who insist that Andy Irons – a true genius of surfing, the only man who could (and for a while, did) eclipse Kelly Slater in the contest arena – died solely of a heart attack. It must have been a freak of nature for no, it's impossible, it couldn't have been drugs, the fiction must be maintained that people as fit as AI do not die in their prime when they're just 32 and with everything to live for. But it seems to me that those who insist on the party line do surfing a disservice. They would do better to celebrate Irons' unquestionable excellence, but acknowledge that he had his problems; in so doing, they may yet help other surfers, and professional sportspeople, from re-enacting his template.

For the record, Irons won the one event that has so far eluded Slater – the Hawaiian Triple Crown. To win one Triple Crown is to gain respect from everyone in surfing; to win four is to achieve legendary status.

Andrew Axel Irons, born on 8 December 2010 – the opening day of that year's Billabong Pipeline Masters – had a father to be proud of.

VEITCH: RIP

A son of Newcastle was one of the most inspirational surfers Europe has ever seen.

A stocky man with blond hair is standing on the edge of a cliff at Tynemouth, Northumberland. It is early in the afternoon on a beautiful, sunny day in April 1991. The North Sea stretches away as far as the eye can see; behind the man are the starkly arresting ruins of Tynemouth Priory and Castle, once one of the most extensive fortified areas in England. The man is a surfer, and on the right day the beach below can serve up decent surf, but he is not checking the surf. Something is wrong. The man – so solidly built that he exudes strength and vitality – is naked. Below him, on the beach and rocks below, are members of the rescue services.

Nigel Veitch once described surfing as "an expression of yourself, an interaction between you and the sea. Like two lovers kissing, it's not the act but the feeling which is important." The poetical nature of the statement reveals much about him. For all the showmanship, for all the charisma, for all that, in the late 1980s, he was once ranked 33 on the Association of Surfing Professionals' World Tour, Veitch – he dropped his Christian name by deed poll – was not a simple man. He painted; he meditated; he wrote poetry – and yet, he was a nightclub bouncer who wanted to be a policeman. He seldom drank – just at Christmas and on New Year's Eve. And whatever he did, he did with a single-mindedness that was perhaps ultimately as unsettling as it was impressive.

But if Veitch's complexity was evident to those who knew him in the North East, his drive was never less than an inspiration. Three surfers in particular were taken under his wing – brothers Jesse and Gabe Davies, and Sam Lamiroy. All would go on to be among the most noted surfers of their generation, with Gabe Davies and Lamiroy amassing multiple British surfing titles and Jesse, albeit that he eschewed the contest scene, establishing himself as one of the country's most respected big wave surfers. All make no bones about the debt they owe Veitch, himself a British Open title winner by the time he was 20.

"Veitch was a legend, no doubt about it," says Lamiroy.

"He taught me so much. He loved nothing better than to push himself, especially in big surf," says Jesse Davies.

Gabe had just entered his teens when Veitch began to encourage his nascent interest in surfing. Along with Jesse, Gabe had already become proficient amid the beachbreak waves of Tynemouth's Longsands beach; it was Veitch who took them off in his car, boards atop the roof, to reveal the jewels of the Northumbria and Yorkshire coastline, reef breaks like the immaculate lefthander at The Cove and, further afield, the reeling perfection of Thurso East on Scotland's north shore. And it was Veitch's stint on the ASP World Tour that showed what grit and determination, allied with talent, can achieve.

"To me, as a young teenager, Veitch was amazing," says Gabe. Now himself at the vanguard of the British tow-in scene and known for having surfed huge swells off the west coast of Ireland, Gabe – so confident in the water – is hesitant when it comes to talking about Veitch. This is not because he doubts his legacy; far from it. It is because of the immense impact the man had on his protégé's life. "He had it all," says Gabe. "He could pull off tricks in small surf and handle himself brilliantly in big waves too."

Few pictures survive of Veitch's time on the World Tour but there is one that is infamous. Veitch is crouching low, wearing blue and red boardshorts, as he speeds through the tube on a white board at massive second reef Pipeline. He looks comfortable and focused, his body somehow taut and yet relaxed as his left hand reaches out to caress the wave. "He was short but had wide shoulders, great core strength and a low centre of gravity – a physique like Tom Carroll's," says Gabe. "He wasn't fazed by big waves at all. To this day, there are very few British surfers who've been as deep as him at second reef Pipe. The image of him in the barrel on that wave stands the test of time. It would be an achievement for any surfer."

Veitch was adopted by Sheila and John Veitch, and grew up in Newcastle. "He was an excellent skateboarder before starting surfing aged 15 alongside the Stores, Hudson and Flannigan families," says Gabe. "As soon as he discovered surfing, it became the main passion in his life."

Newcastle Breweries recognised Veitch's talent, and provided sufficient sponsorship for him to tackle the World Tour in 1986. If the man with the Brown Ale logo made for an unlikely participant at the elite level, he more than held his own, often making it through the trials to compete in the main event against the likes of Carroll and the three-time world champion Tom Curren. Finishing 33rd was no mean feat for a British surfer; having the commitment, drive and imagination even to dare to compete was perhaps even more remarkable.

But in Britain, after a heady year travelling and surfing the world's best waves, Veitch's life seemed to stall. He had sustained a serious knee injury while on Oahu's North Shore, and back on home soil his recuperation was dealt a blow when Newcastle Breweries decided to withdraw its sponsorship. The man who, according to Gabe, "was like a magnet, he was so full of life and enthusiasm", became withdrawn and reserved. He still surfed, and he still commanded the respect of the North East's hardy crew of locals, as well as the UK's surfing cognoscenti. But something was wrong. Veitch was not himself. Nevertheless, there was no clue as to quite how depressed he had become.

"I was walking home from school one April afternoon," recalls Gabe, his voice again growing distant, "when I could see a commotion at the castle. There were so many people milling around that I knew at once that something major had happened. But I didn't think it could be to do with Veitch."

Gabe, along with Jesse and Lamiroy, and any number of other people who knew Veitch, was devastated when he found out that his hero had dived headlong from the cliff edge, to die on the rocks 100 ft below.

"People have said that he was on drugs, or that he'd been drinking, but it's nonsense," says Gabe. "Veitch was the cleanest person I knew. He was super fit and healthy."

But Veitch had fallen into debt – life on the tour was not cheap, and his sponsors' support didn't cover all the costs it entailed – and it seems that he had fallen out with his girlfriend at the time. Exactly why he took his life that sunny, ostensibly benign April day will forever be a mystery, but that Veitch is a British surfing legend is beyond doubt. As Gabe says, "The determination with which he lived his life and the way he overcame adversity from such an unlikely beginning, to live and fulfil his dreams, is inspiration in its purest form. In his final action it seems that Veitch made his mind up and committed himself as he always did. There was no way he was pulling back from his last drop. He was desperately missed."

Sheila and John asked Gabe and Jesse to scatter Veitch's ashes in the North Sea, which the boys duly did. Jesse himself never moved away from Tynemouth, while Gabe, after a prolonged spell in France, recently returned to live in his hometown, a place where he fell under the tutelage of the late, great Nigel Veitch, the man who lit the touch paper for so many British – and European – surfers, a man who once said "one of the great things about surfing is that there is no wrong or right". Tynemouth is a place where Gabe may well run into Sheila. "She was always a great supporter of the local surf scene, and she still is," he says. "She often comes to contests and surf film screenings. The story of the lad she raised shows that it's not the time you're in this world but the number of souls you touch, that shows a life of true quality, well-lived."

QED

Saudade for Angus Chater.

In 1984, QED Publishing Ltd released a book called *The Windsurfing Funboard Handbook*. It was a 'how to' guide to the new sport of wavesailing, which in the early 80s, saw windsurfing evolve from a flat water pursuit to something which was every bit as adrenalin-charged as traditional surfing.

Thanks to pioneers such as Robbie Naish, Jurgen Honscheid, Fraser Black and Ken Winner, windsurfers began to ride waves like conventional surfers, the difference being that they could jump them too, sometimes even inverting board and rig before landing upright and powering off to hit the next wave. Today, the upside-down jump is one of a proficient wavesailor's bag of tricks, but back then it was about as spectacular as windsurfing could be. There were few better exponents of it, and all the other radical moves which windsurfers were trying out, than Angus Chater, the co-author of QED's seminal book.

Chater is pictured on the inside dust jacket of the book. He is smiling at the camera (perhaps one operated by Clive Boden, a professional photographer and Chater's co-author), with the deep blue of the sea in the background. It looks as if he is wearing a harness, used by windsurfers to take the strain out of controlling their rigs. Otherwise, his bare chest is visible. It is a deep bronze, as if Chater has lived in the Tropics all his life. His hair is straight and bleach-blond; he looks exuberant and happy.

Chater hailed from Dorset. He was brought up mainly in landlocked Derbyshire, and despite the fact that he travelled with his parents to Libya, Cyprus and Sudan there is something peculiarly English about the way he looks in his photograph in *The Windsurfing Funboard Handbook*. It is almost as if he is shy, unassuming, humble; the kind of man who would be happier behind the lens than in front of it. Certainly, Chater went on to blaze a trail not merely as a wavesailor, but as a photographer too. Along with Fraser Black, he was one of the first English windsurfers to decamp to Hawaii, but as much as he windsurfed – and surfed – Chater established a formidable reputation as a photographer.

"As far I know, Angus was the first person to put a camera on the end of a boom and use it in the water," says Alex Williams, the veteran surf photographer. Williams knew Chater well as the pair would often be in Hawaii at the same time. "Angus went there in the early 80s and just before his visa was about to expire, met a lady called Pam. They got married. It was a marriage of convenience, yes, but then they fell in love. Angus stayed and built a name for himself as a wavesailor, and also became a good, solid surfer. He didn't rip, but he could handle Sunset at any size. Life seemed to be perfect for him."

Pam picks up the story. "Angus was a sports commentator on the popular television programme *The Wide World of Sports* for two Ocean Pacific [OP] windsurfing events in Hawaii. He also modelled for various sportswear companies, was in TV commercials and became a member of the Screen Actors Guild. We actually got married so that he could join the Guild and get paid for the commercials."

A conversation between Williams and Chater, as they drove away from Diamond Head (the world-class windsurfing location on Oahu), inspired Chater's move into surfing photography. "We were chatting away when Angus said that he didn't know what to do with himself when the wind disappeared in the Hawaiian winter. He could go surfing on the North Shore but needed something else. By then, he'd become a decent surfer and was also a good photographer. I suggested that he put the two things together. His skills would mean that by rights, he'd be able to take some great surfing shots."

And so it proved – in spades, for Chater also brought his windsurfing background to bear. In adapting a windsurfing boom (a part of the rig) and making his own camera housings, he displayed a blend of creativity and practicality that was matched by bravery. Chater was, according to Williams, "possibly the first person to swim out at Pipeline with a pole camera". His innovation and talent mean that Chater was soon "getting shots that no one else was getting, revolutionary part under the water and part over the water images. He was setting the standard".

Soon enough, Chater had an eight-page spread in *Surfer* magazine. He was sponsored by Rip Curl, Neil Pryde and Sea Panther. He would commentate at events for OP. The young man from Dorset seemed set to live the dream in paradise.

But an incident at Sunset changed everything. Williams explains that "Chater was surfing the inside bowl when the lip hit him and crunched his face into his knee. He was knocked out. Barton Lynch, Mark Occhilupo and Dan Merkel got him to the shore, but his heart didn't start beating again until he was in the helicopter on the way to hospital. He was out for eight minutes."

Williams heard about the accident from afar. A few months later, he was in Hawaii. "I went to see Angus at his house at Lanakai. He wasn't himself. He was always so positive, and now had terrible mood swings. I remember seeing him working on a VW Rabbit, then beating its bonnet in rage with a bamboo cane, like John Cleese in *Fawlty Towers*." Chater had separated from Pam, and was drinking a lot, too, "Every evening he'd down too many beers. He used to just have the one, but now it was a few."

But still, romance was in the air. Just before he left, Williams heard Chater "saying a lot of things that were very dark", but he felt buoyed by the fact that his friend was talking of moving to Maui and starting afresh with a new girlfriend.

It wasn't to be. In July 1987, Chater drove his car to a lighthouse near Hookipa on Maui, taped up the windows and ran a tube from the exhaust pipe to the driver's side window. He turned the ignition on and asphyxiated himself.

"It was tragic," says Williams. "Angus was always so vibrant, so full of life."

The Windsurfing Funboard Handbook is still to be found on windsurfers' shelves, in their garages and even on Amazon. Its guidance on moves like carve and duck gybes, water starts and jumps, is as accurate today as it was in 1984. The ghost of Angus Chater pops up on windsurfing forums from time to time; his memory enters Alex Williams' mind often.

Pam looks back on her time with Chater with affection and melancholy. The Portuguese have a term for looking back both wistfully and sadly, with deep and unrequited emotion for that which is lost. It is *'saudade'*. Pam's comments are perhaps the definition of saudade:

"We never lived apart after our marriage until he left for Maui. His affair lasted all of about three months, and after moving in with her for one week he called and said he wanted to come home. Afraid that he was jumping to conclusions, I asked him to stay in Maui for a month just to be sure that he truly wanted to come home. He agreed, and moved in with Klaus Zimmerman. He wrote to me every day and sent flowers twice a week. The week before he was to come home, he committed suicide on 4 July. It was such a shock since things seemed to be going so well. Suicide is such an insidious thing to do. All these years later I have not formed another relationship, nor have I dated. He broke many hearts that day. In his final letter to me, he asked me not to be mad at him, and to forgive him for his actions. I guess I have, but I still can't get past it. I will love him forever."

As for QED – *'quod erat demonstrandum'*, in Latin – it means 'as was to be expected'. It is generally placed at the end of a mathematical or philosophical position which has been conclusively proved by an argument. There is little in Angus Chater's life and death to warrant a pat 'QED', save perhaps: "Surfing at Sunset. QED."

THE PETERSON PROBLEM

How do we make sense of the late, great Michael Peterson?

On the evening of 9 August 1983, a year after he had given up surfing, Michael Peterson was arrested after a high-speed police chase that culminated in the closure of Story Bridge, Brisbane. By then aged 30, MP – as he was nicknamed by Peter Townend ('PT') another great Australian surfer – was revered as Australia's greatest surfer. He had pulled up at the roadside in the Beenleigh suburb of Brisbane to sleep, only to wake to the sound of a police siren. Startled, he chose to speed away rather than slumber on and, as was apparently his intention, go windsurfing at Noosa the following day. The police car had been travelling in the opposite direction, but turned to give pursuit.

'The Chase', as it became known in surfing circles, morphed into something straight out of Hollywood. Some 20 police cars followed Peterson, whose car mounted a pavement at one point and nearly killed some pedestrians; a further 15 police cars formed the roadblock on the bridge. Upon his arrest, Peterson is said to have told the police that he was a CIA agent and that he was being followed by Russian spies.

According to another account, however, Peterson told the arresting officer that he had successfully evaded Martians. The discrepancy is typical in the life story of a man who, in his prime, lit up surfing as few have done before or since, but whose descent into drug abuse and eventual diagnosis as a paranoid schizophrenic is the stuff of tragedy.

Michael Peterson was born and raised in the beachside suburb of Kirra on Queensland's Gold Coast. His mother, Joan, ran a pool hall. She had the sole care of Peterson, his younger brother Tommy, and his two sisters. The family's existence was not comfortable. Money was always tight, and the first surfboards ridden by Peterson and his brother were those which had been abandoned or lost by other surfers. Later, the pair began to shape their own boards – it was cheaper than buying them – but in 1968, Joan promised her elder son a new board if he won a local surf life-saving championship.

Peterson duly obliged, making for the first of many competition successes. Having dropped out of school aged 16, he signalled his intent to make a lasting impression as a surfer by winning one of Australia's iconic contests in 1970, held annually at Bell's Beach, Victoria. In the same year, he came third in the Australian National Titles; in 1971 he won what was to be the first of three Queensland state titles.

By 1972, Peterson had become the national surfing champion in Australia, an achievement that he replicated in 1974. He also proved himself at the surf breaks on the north shore of the Hawaiian island of Oahu, although he had only visited Hawaii three times, and made a telling appearance in one of surfing's most influential films, *Morning of the Earth.* Directed by Alby Falzon, the 1972 film featured a number of the era's best surfers, including Hawaii's Gerry Lopez and fellow Australians Nat Young and Terry Fitzgerald, but it was Peterson who stole the show. Lean and tall, with his long hair flying as he carved through turns, Peterson brought an exquisite sense of rhythm to surfing. It was epitomised in a still from the film, known simply as 'the cutback', which became one of the sport's iconic images.

But as much as he was a dynamic, fluid and innovative force in the water, Peterson found life on land difficult. Always a man of few words, he would appear by turns shy and surly, all the more so if he had just won a contest. His temper would explode for no apparent reason, especially in arguments with his younger brother. As Matt Warshaw recounts in *The Encyclopedia of Surfing* "... younger brother Tom became one of Queensland's best surfboard shapers ... Fighting in the water once as teenagers, Michael ripped Tom's board away from him and paddled it out past the shark nets; Tom then swam to shore, opened the hood of Michael's car, and hurled his brother's distributor and battery into the surf". He might lament to an Australian magazine that he did his best to be like everyone else, "but it's hard", but MP's problems only got worse. He once hid in the car park behind the beach after taking his third consecutive Bell's Beach title, believing the crowd would assault him if he accepted his winnings. And in his last contest, he competed against Mark Richards (subsequently a four-times world champion) while high on drugs.

In that event, the 1977 Stubbies pro at Burleigh Heads on the Gold Coast, Peterson vanquished Richards, but he was unable to beat his demons. He became a heavy drug user and only sporadically surfed until abandoning the sport altogether in 1982. Then came The Chase, a sentence of a year's imprisonment, and institutionalisation. By 1984, Peterson had been diagnosed as a paranoid schizophrenic.

Peterson lived for much of the remainder of his life with his mother. Medication to control his schizophrenia meant that his weight ballooned and he was seldom seen in public. He co-operated with noted Australian surfing writer Sean Doherty for the publication of the latter's 2004 biography, *MP: The Life of Michael Peterson*, but his friends' hopes that he might one day return to surfing were destined to remain in the realms of fantasy.

MP died of a heart attack on 29 March 2012. Obituaries appeared not merely in surfing magazines but in reputable newspapers around the world (a version of this piece was published by *The Times*), and online surf forums were full of eulogies for the late, great, Queensland surfer. Doubtless this is because, along with Miki Dora, Peterson was the quintessential outlaw surfer; the man of few words, enigmatic drives and uncertain temperament whose ability in the sea was, until he decided to abandon it, a thing of poetry.

Curiously, Michael Peterson is also the real name of the notorious British convict whose alias is Charles Bronson, a man who has spent the past 38 years in prison, 33 of which have been in solitary confinement. Making sense of Bronson's life, one whose offences include armed robbery, grievous bodily harm, wounding, wounding with intent, false imprisonment, blackmail and threatening to kill, is no easier than assessing that of Michael Peterson the surfer, but if the two men were born in the same year, if both were prone to serious mental disturbances and if both had films and books written about their extraordinary inability to adhere to rules and convention, there is a key difference: MP left a legacy, one of beauty, sunshine and freedom.

PART THREE

When the Big Stuff Bites

A BITE OUT OF BURLE

Carlos Burle is one of the world's best big wave surfers. He knows from personal experience that in his game, you have to pay your dues. In 2003, he did just that, and then some, at Jaws.

Hailing from Recife, Pernambuco, in the north-east of Brazil, Carlos Burle first came to Hawaii in the winter of 1986/87. Since then, the Brazilian has returned to spend five months every year, each November to March, on the North Shore of Oahu. He has surfed any number of Hawaiian breaks and plenty elsewhere too, earning a reputation as one of the very best big wave surfers in the world. Triumphs include big wave competition wins at Todos Santos and Maverick's – the latter seeing Burle ride a wave which, at 68 ft, was then the world record for the biggest wave surfed.

The son of a chicken farmer, Burle's exploits have enabled him to live a radically different life to his father. Burle splits his time between Hawaii and Brazil and just about anywhere on the planet where the surf is pumping. Sponsorship deals with the likes of Red Bull, Bridgestone and Finisterre help him travel to Teahupoo, to Ireland, to Chile, to Peru – wherever he needs to be to ride heavy, gnarly and downright dangerous surf. Quietly spoken and humble, Burle is described by Grant Baker (himself a highly regarded big wave surfer) as "the most intelligent person I have surfed big waves with. He makes no mistakes and still surfs the biggest waves of any day."

But in Burle's profession, you have to pay your dues. In 2001, he emerged with broken vertebrae from a hold-down at one of the most photographed big wave spots of them all – Backdoor Pipeline, on the Hawaiian island of Oahu. That was bad, but worse was to come. In January 2003, Burle came within an inch of being the first person to drown at Jaws.

"I was tow-surfing with Eraldo Gueiros, my regular tow partner," he recalls. "The day was sunny and super clear and even better, the line-up was uncrowded. There weren't many tow teams in the water. The surf was big – around 60 ft – but the swell had picked up unexpectedly and only a few guys had managed to get organised to be there."

Ever since Laird Hamilton and the 'Strapped Crew', including the likes of Buzzy Kerbox, Dave Kalama and Darrick Doerner, started towing in at Jaws in the early 1990s, the monumental right-hander is generally packed whenever it breaks. So busy is its line-up, that elite surfers have even called for some form of regulation to limit the numbers of putative hellmen who arrive to try and chalk up 'Jaws: ridden' on their list of surf scalps. To find Jaws relatively uncrowded on a 60 ft day was, for Burle and Gueiros, a slice of great good fortune.

So too, were Burle's first waves that day. "I'd had about 10 waves, and was feeling good, having had a lot of time to train that year. Winter 2002/03 was really consistent and Eraldo and I were out practising every day, but not just in average surf – in solid, big, decent waves. I felt in good shape, fit and strong, and my vertebrae, which I'd broken two years before, had healed well."

So far, so good. Burle was experiencing big wave bliss, when everything comes together: the surf, the preparation, the equipment, not to mention fitness and trust in one's tow partner. Throw in a bright, sun-kissed day and all was well with the world.

Except that bliss, as those who seek it know all too well, doesn't last forever. "I was on a high after a nice tube ride but then it all went wrong.

Very wrong. Maybe I overestimated my ability, maybe I didn't assess the risks correctly. I don't know. But I'll never forget what happened next."

Burle found himself speeding down the face of a massive wave, about half way to the safety of the channel, when instead of continuing to ride the wave (so that he would end up beyond the impact zone) he kicked out, towards the peak. What he saw next was not welcome. "A massive set from the west was heading towards me. I decided to try and make it through by paddling my tow board over the first wave. That was a bad decision. There was no way I could make it. The lip rose and started to break and took me down over the falls. I got twisted so badly that I heard a crack, even as I was being smashed around by the white water."

Fortunately, Eraldo made it to Burle to rescue him – but not before he had been hit by two more waves. But as he clambered onto the sled of his partner's jetski, Burle knew things were awry. "I remember shouting to Eraldo 'I've broken my back!' Then I just lay face down on the sled. I couldn't move at all."

Burle was conscious, but the pain was immense. "From the sled, to the seat of the jetski, to the ambulance and then to the hospital, I just stayed in the same position. The pain was beyond anything I had ever felt before; way, way worse. I was terrified that I would be paralysed. Eventually, I had some X-rays, but it wasn't until I'd had them done that I was allowed any painkillers."

The X-rays confirmed that Burle had broken his sacrum, the large, triangular bone at the base of the spine. That, though, wasn't the end of it.

"After a week, as the pain in my back reduced a little, I started to notice that my left leg was in terrible pain. I spent a month calling my doctor in Brazil, asking what the problem might be, all the while dragging myself around my house in Hawaii on crutches. I was finally well enough to fly back to Brazil. The trip home on the plane was hideous, the worst ever, with so much pain all the way. But in Brazil I had an MRI scan. It's much more specific than an X-ray, and allowed the doctors to see the extent of the damage. Not only had the sacrum cracked, but I'd also broken the lumbar vertebrae at L1 and the head of my femur on the left side. That was actually the worst area affected.

If it didn't heal well I would have to go through surgery and have it replaced with a prosthetic part."

If that had happened, Burle's days as a big wave surfer could well have been numbered. He knew he was lucky to avoid paralysis, but recovery was tough. "I had many black days when I wondered if I'd ever get fully better. I felt a lot of pressure and doubt, in the media especially, and worried whether my sponsors would stick by me. But they did, and I kept my focus and worked really hard, especially in physiotherapy. I'd lost weight – I went down to 61 kg – but I worked out so much that I went up to 72 kg. And by then, I knew I could do it. I knew I'd make it back to being able to do what I used to do, and what I love doing."

In all, the accident saw Burle on crutches for four months. Another six months elapsed before he was able to return to the big wave scene. Now in his mid-40s, Burle says he takes great care to balance the risks and rewards of big wave surfing: "I don't want another bad accident. There's too much stress!" But the man who is nicknamed 'The Jackal' seems to have got the balance right: in 2010, seven years after the incident that could have easily seen him paralysed or even killed, Burle was crowned champion of the Big Wave World Tour.

Meanwhile, despite exacting a toll from many other surfers, Jaws has yet to make any of them pay the ultimate price. But a benign wave this isn't, and, as Carlos Burle knows better than anyone, those who underestimate it do so at their peril.

PEOPLE IN CAR CRASHES DON'T STOP DRIVING

Shark attacks are a risk at some of the world's most beautiful breaks. One teenager's response when the worst happened is so exceptional that it bears repeating.

It's the last morning of October 2003 on the Hawaiian island of Kauai. As she does just about every day, a 13-year-old girl wakes up early and full of energy. She's surf-obsessed and can't wait to get in the water, not just because she lives for surfing, but because she has dreams of making it as a pro too. Surfing, for this teenager, is already a way of life but she's so good that the chances are that surfing is also how she's going to make her living.

Bethany Hamilton, the daughter of fanatical surfing parents, is ready for action before sunrise. She and her mother Cheri head off in the pre-dawn semi-darkness to check the surf at Pauaeaka. It's still dark when they get there but, ever eager, Bethany jumps out of the car and runs to the beach. Initially, she can't see the surf, but soon there's enough light to discern that today she and her mother won't be surfing Pauaeaka. There are waves, but they're dumping over the coral reef rather than peeling to offer surfable rides. Bethany is not the only one who's disappointed. Her mother sighs and says "I guess we should head back. Maybe the surf will come up tomorrow."

But as Cheri starts the car and sets off for their home, inspiration strikes Bethany. "Let's just check out Tunnels beach," she says. Cheri is happy to oblige. She spins the car around and the pair are soon at Tunnels, a reef break a short distance from Pauaeaka. Bethany jumps out and walks along the sandy path to the beach. Again, she is dismayed. "Nothing doing," she says to herself. She's home-schooled, and so trudges back to her mother's car resigned to returning home to study.

Fate, or the surf gods, or God – Bethany and her family are devout Christians – had other ideas. Cue the arrival of Bethany's best friend, Alana Blanchard with her brother Byron and father Holt. Bethany grew up surfing with Alana, and a momentum seizes the quartet despite the lacklustre surf. "Can I stay, Mom?" asks Bethany. "We think we'll paddle out for some small waves." Cheri is tirelessly supportive of her daughter. She agrees but opts to head home, and so adds the kind of redundant comment irresistible to doting parents the world over. "Just make sure that Holt brings you home."

At 6am Bethany enters the warm water and paddles the 500 yards to the line-up. While Tunnels can be crowded on good days, today the lacklustre waves mean that Bethany and her friends have got the place to themselves. They're alone, free to enjoy the beauty of the set-up: the sea which is surprisingly clear despite heavy overnight rain, and the sense of freshness and exhilaration which comes of an early morning surf. Alone, that is, save for the marine life. And at Tunnels, so named because it is a barrel ride paradise, that marine life includes an awful lot of sharks: hammerheads, tiger and reef sharks abound. Some say that they're most dangerous in April and October, either early in the morning or just before sunrise. It's early morning, on the last day of October and Halloween night looms.

For Kauai's surfers, as for those in many other sun-kissed surf kingdoms, sharks are a fact of life. They're always there, in the depths, *somewhere*. Sometimes they're clearly visible, as surfers sit on their boards waiting for waves. They cruise elegantly, indifferently, implacably, just a few yards beneath the surface; the surfer who sees one hopes it'll cruise on away, somewhere else. But on the last day of October in 2003, a 13 ft tiger shark elected not to cruise on away somewhere else. Instead, it decided to attack Bethany Hamilton, ripping off her left arm beneath the shoulder.

The savagery of the attack was startling – as clinically brutal as anything the most twisted sadist could ever devise. Worse, the shock and agony were instantaneous. Blood poured from Bethany's severed limb, turning the sea crimson. Just about anyone else might have died of shock there and then, not least from fear of a second attack. Not Bethany. As the Blanchards heard her screams and paddled frantically towards her, she somehow stayed calm. Likewise, as they manoeuvred her and her broken board – the shark had bitten a 17-inch chunk out of it – to the shallow water sanctuary of the reef, she managed to keep her cool.

But the flow of blood was relentless. At this rate, Bethany would surely die and Holt Blanchard knew this. Rallying Byron and Alana, he and his children paddled Bethany from the coral reef to the shore of Tunnels Beach as quickly as possible. Once there, Holt fashioned a tourniquet from a surfboard leash and tied it around the stump of Bethany's arm. It was as rudimentary – almost futile – as could be, but at least it was something. Meanwhile, as an incredible 60 per cent of Bethany's blood seeped from her wound, Byron ran to his father's pick-up truck to find a phone. He dialed 911 for an ambulance, but Holt knew they couldn't wait. Within minutes he had put Bethany into the pick-up, and set off at high speed to Wilcox Memorial Hospital, one of the two hospitals on Kauai.

Tom Hamilton was already at the hospital – but he wasn't expecting his daughter. The man who hailed originally from Ocean City, New Jersey – a man so dedicated to surfing that he would paddle out to his favourite Ocean City surf spot, Tenth Street, even when ice and snow lay all around – had just had a spinal tap prior to a scheduled knee operation. As he lay waiting, his legs anaesthetized, a nurse entered and told the orthopaedic surgeon, Dr David Rovinsky, that the room was needed for an emergency. It was a 13-year-old female shark attack victim.

Fast forward six years. Astonishingly, Bethany – who was surfing again less than a month after the trauma of that Halloween day – went on to turn pro in 2007. She rose through the ranks of the women's World Qualifying Series and onto the Association Surfing Professionals Tour, placing in the top three of many elite events and acquitting herself with skill, grace and aplomb. She even went on to tow-surf the notorious big wave break of Jaws on the island of Maui. Her story is known the world over thanks to a book, *Soul Surfer*, and a film of the same name. But how did she do it?

"I learnt to surf again by popping up using my right arm, placing it in the middle of the board. And for duck-diving, my dad made a handle that's in the middle of the board. I was competing again by January, three months after the attack." Moreover, she adds "I learnt to counter the lack of one arm in turns," and that "God allowed the attack to happen for beautiful reasons. A lot of beautiful things have happened because of it."

And as for sharks, they're not a problem. "I've been surfing again plenty of times at Tunnels," says Bethany. "I never think about whether there might be any sharks around. It's not a big deal. After all, people in car crashes don't stop driving."

BARE HANDS AND BOMBS

Tony Butt may be one of big wave surfing's unsung heroes, but he's more than paid his dues.

"A lot of things have happened to me at Meñakoz. Not all of them have been positive."

Tony Butt smiles as he describes his love affair with one of Europe's premier waves, a break that he first surfed in 1991 on his fourth trip to Spain. "I'd heard rumours about Meñakoz but didn't know much about it, save that it could apparently hold waves of over 20 ft. That and the fact that it was only surfed by a handful of locals. It sounded perfect."

Butt, an oceanographer and author, started surfing on England's south coast in 1972. By the mid-1980s, he had gravitated to big wave surfing, as much because of a loathing for crowded line-ups as for the sheer thrill. "I hate crowds and I'm not competitive," says Butt, a wiry and bearded man in his early 50s. "I'd heard that in big wave surfing there was a sense of camaraderie, a feeling of community among surfers; that they would share waves rather than drop in and snake each other. That was much more my kind of thing."

The man who originally hails from the relatively quiescent waters of Bournemouth thus embarked on a search for big waves that would see him travel to Hawaii, where he surfed Sunset at size, and also to Peru and Chile, where he surfed Pico Alto and Punta de Lobos, before the first of many trips to South Africa. Butt has since made an annual pilgrimage to surf South Africa's most challenging big waves – the likes of Dungeons and Sunset Reef – but those early trips to Spain were to prove life-changing.

"On that trip, with just a couple of mates, we drove back through the Basque Country during a huge swell. Mundaka was closing out from end to end. We took the coast road up through Gipuzcoa and on towards France. We saw perfect left-handers breaking at the bottom of inaccessible cliffs, a right-hand point break at one side of a large bay, and several huge peaks breaking just a few metres from the road. The strange thing was that we didn't see one other surfer."

The lack of a crowd and the quality of the surf persuaded Butt to journey again to northern Spain. "I took myself to Galicia for the winter of 1992 in a van and again with two friends. We started in Baiona, just north of the Portuguese border, and worked our way around the coast, part of which is aptly named *La Costa de la Muerte* ('The Coast of the Dead'). We didn't score too many killer waves, and we did get very wet – it rains all the time in Galicia – but things improved when we made our way into Asturias. We came across a rather flat section of north-east facing coastline. There was a fantastic right-hander there which we called 'The Hollow Right'. And yet again, there were no crowds. It was bliss for two weeks, and for the next five years we would return and surf it on our own. Then the locals discovered it and gave it their own name: *La Machacona* – 'The Crusher'."

By the time the Spanish had experienced the joy and pain of La Machacona, Butt was living full-time in Euskadi. The reason was Meñakoz. "I became obsessed with it," he says.

For the past 15 years and counting, the natural footer Butt has been a fixture in the line-up at Meñakoz. The break may be close to the less than picturesque town of Sopelana, but its setting is stupendous. Huge cliffs tower over the sea, and with parking almost on the cliff edge, the heaving right-handers of Meñakoz can be watched as if from an amphitheatre. Today, when Meñakoz is working, crowds will line the cliffs, but it wasn't always so.

"Although there was already an established local crew there, most of them had full-time jobs. For the first few years, on a lot of the big days I'd go out there on my own, wishing someone else would join me," says Butt, echoing the experience of Californian legend Jeff Clark, who surfed Maverick's on his own for some 15 years. "Even some of the local surfers started asking me what it was like. I was always happy to see one or two more of them in the line-up."

Over time, Butt has noted a curious pattern. "Whenever I move to a new area or start surfing a new spot, I've noticed that there seems to be a lot of interest from my friends at the beginning, but this always seems to wear off, and I end up back on my own again. This has happened several times, and is definitely the case with Meñakoz. At the beginning my mates from the UK would come down there with me. For a few years they would come and visit me, but this eventually wore off. Then, when I started going down to South Africa every year, for the first few years I'd have somebody with me, but then the same thing happened. In the end I always end up surfing on my own." He muses that his friends' steady disappearance from spots that he discovers, might be because "they've concluded that I'm crazy, or reckon they'll have a better time in Indo" – a theory that gains credibility when Butt also confesses that he has lately taken to surfing another highly dangerous wave in his adopted country. "The locals all knew about it, but I was the first person to surf it, eight years ago" he says, adding phlegmatically that even now "it's a very tricky proposition. I'm out there most of the time on my own. I'm the only surfer within about 100 km who regularly surfs this spot."

But surfing any big wave break, whether those that Butt would prefer to keep secret or known spots, is never free from danger, albeit that it took a while for Butt to be on the receiving end of a beating at Meñakoz. "I made plenty of mistakes in the early days. I used to paddle out on all tides but then I realised that it was only really good at high tide. There was never anyone around during the week at the beginning, which was great in one way, worrying in another, but nothing went wrong in the beginning either. I even began to think that the wave's reputation was exaggerated. But then a guy broke seven ribs when he got pummelled onto the rocks, then another bloke broke his leg. And then came the first of my nailings at Meñakoz. My leash got caught on some rocks and I was worked onto the cliffs. It took me ages to get out. When I made it to the car I realised that I was in a lot of pain. It turned out that I'd broken my foot."

The summary of Meñakoz on the surf forecasting site Magic Seaweed turns out to have an up-close and personal basis – Butt wrote it, originally for the Stormrider Europe guide: "World-class, highly dangerous big-wave spot. One of the most powerful, regularly-surfed waves in Europe. Starts breaking properly at about 12 ft. Hazards include razor-sharp rocks, very strong rips, shifting peaks, two-wave hold-downs, broken boards and broken bones."

On another occasion, a fall saw Butt hit his head on some rocks; this resulted in 16 staples to staunch the resulting wound. Then there was a two-wave hold down, the kind of thing which, says Butt, he thought "only happened at a place like Maverick's". He has lost a board and been the victim of rogue sets which swing in, away from the peak. "It's a very demanding place to surf. You have to keep paddling constantly, chasing peaks and avoiding wide, in-swinging sets. You will definitely get caught inside and you will definitely not enjoy being worked." But that said, one thing is always comforting about Meñakoz: this is a paddle-in only wave. "Thankfully, tow-surfing is not allowed at Meñakoz," confirms Butt, who once found himself short-listed as a potential European entrant for the Quiksilver in Memory of Eddie Aikau Invitational, the prestigious big wave event held at Waimea Bay, but only when the surf exceeds 20 ft.

Butt's antipathy to tow-in surfing is as ingrained as the way that some people like dogs but hate cats. "Fumes, noise, jetskis, ropes – no, not my thing at all," he says. Butt is a purist, an ideologist among surfers, a man who endorses long-time Maverick's local Mark 'Doc' Renneker's views. "Renneker was an outspoken critic of tow-surfing but for a long time he was abused as a dinosaur. But things have turned full circle and the Doc is having the last laugh. Tow-surfing may have been all the rage at a number of big wave spots since the mid-1990s but now people are paddling into what was famously described as 'the unridden realm'. It was to ride these waves – breaks like Outer Log

Cabins on Oahu, or Jaws on Maui – that tow-surfing was invented, but now the super-elite among big wave surfers have turned against the crowding caused by tow-in surfing and the fact that many tow-in crews have scant real experience of big wave surfing. The example of veteran North Shore lifeguard and big wave legend Darrick Doerner is typical. He took up tow-surfing precisely to get away from the crowds at Waimea and Sunset Beach, but ended up being haunted by them."

That tow-surfing is no longer uncritically endorsed by the big wave community is evidenced not merely by those Butt characterises as the 'super-elite' – men like Shane Dorian, Greg Long, Grant 'Twiggy' Baker and Peter Mel, who have recently paddled into bombs at Jaws and Cortes Bank – but by the organisers of an annual tow-in event at Nelscott Reef in Oregon. As Butt puts it: "Nelscott is considered to be the ideal tow-in wave, and every year a tow-surfing contest is held there. However, the organizers insist that 'Big wave credentials are established by paddling big waves, not by buying a jet ski' and have started holding a paddle event just to make sure contestants know what they are doing before they tow. The paddle session in 2010 got just as much, if not more publicity, than the tow event." Another key turning point came in July 2008, when the Big Wave Africa contest was held in solid 25 ft to 30 ft Dungeons. "The event took place in conditions which previously had always been considered too big and gnarly to paddle," says Butt, who was invited to the same contest in 2002. "It helped set in motion the change in attitude that now sees every big wave surfer worthy of the name seek to paddle into waves with his or her bare hands wherever possible, rather than tow-surf them."

Ironically, Butt's satisfaction in seeing the renaissance of big wave paddle-in surfing is tinged with frustration, for now his passion for extreme conditions has been put on hold. The reason? A fall – at Meñakoz. "I fell backwards on a big wave and landed hard on my neck," he reveals. Subsequent pain and neurological problems led Butt to seek an MRI scan. The result, according to a Spanish neurosurgeon, is a badly damaged cervical spine. Surgery is possible, and may well prevent further deterioration, but whether Butt will be able to return to big waves has been questioned by doctors and physiotherapists. Certainly, surfing a demanding wave like Meñakoz after spinal surgery would not be encouraged by members of the medical profession.

Butt is worried about what he would do if he couldn't surf places like Meñakoz and another of his cherished Spanish breaks, a giant point break known as *La Verdad* ('The Truth'). "The winter of 2009/10 was epic for La Verdad. I surfed some of the biggest waves of my life there. It's a pretty extreme surf spot – not for everybody. For a start, the wave breaks in front of a nasty cliff and the only safe access point is three kilometres away. Nobody has got in trouble there yet so we don't know what the consequences are. But the experience of being out there is worth it, even if you only catch one wave. I don't know what I'd do if I couldn't paddle into waves there, or at Meñakoz, or once a year for my month-long stay in South Africa. My doctor finds it all baffling; he reckons I should just find something else to do. But my whole life is surfing. I wouldn't even be there speaking to him in Spanish if it wasn't for surfing. My job is wrapped up in surfing; I met my wife through surfing. Surfing is everything to me."

Perhaps though, the answer lies in one of Butt's earliest memories of surfing in Spain. He was in Galicia surfing a wave he had christened 'Chestnut Reef', simply because there was a chestnut tree nearby. It was time to come in after a few hours' surfing a "bouncy, shoulder-less wave; really just a take-off but still, I was stoked to be the first to surf it". Butt spotted a sandy beach, and paddled for it, thinking it would make for an easier way to come in than returning to his original jump-off point.

"As I got out of the water, a local farmer cutting the grass with a giant scythe, stopped and looked up at me. I guess he didn't have a clue what the hell I was doing. I needed to get back to the main road where I had parked my car, so asked him if he could explain to me, *en Castellano, por favor*, how to get there."

Answering in Gallego, a Latin-based language that sounds like Spanish but bears a close relation to Portuguese, the man told Butt to go along the railway line and cross a bridge. "I said 'What about the trains?' to which the man merely said 'Today is Tuesday'. I must have looked bewildered, because he then added, looking at me as if I was an idiot 'Don't you know? There are no trains on Tuesdays!' I thanked him and continued on my way. When I looked back he was once again absorbed in his work. I couldn't help but wonder what was going through his mind. He didn't seem even vaguely surprised that I had emerged from the sea wearing a black rubber suit and a white plastic helmet, and carrying a fish-like object. He was more shocked that I didn't know there were no trains on Tuesdays. I had seen this kind of thing before – an almost blatant acceptance of the totally incomprehensible. Apparently, in this part of the world, it is quite normal."

For many, spinal surgery might mean an acceptance of gentle gardening as the extent of one's future physical endeavours. But that Butt – Britain's answer to Jeff Clark, an underground charger if ever there was one – will give up big wave surfing seems inconceivable. This is a man whose familiarity with the apparently incomprehensible will surely see him once again paddling into bombs with his bare hands – albeit with a recalibrated neck.

THE WHITE ZONE

When Andrew Cotton bagged the wave of the day at Mullaghmore Head in March 2012, everything went white. It could have been worse.

Andrew Cotton's memory of one of the biggest waves ever ridden off the coast of Ireland is not extensive.

"I thought it was done," says the 32-year-old regular footer from Braunton, North Devon. "I'd just done a mid-face fade and a turn, and had been hit by a little bit of spit. But then everything went white. It was like a car crash. The impact felt very still, almost peaceful. But I can't remember much more than that. It may have been one of the worst beatings I've ever had but I'm not really sure."

What is certain about Cotton's first wave of an epic session at Mullaghmore Head in County Donegal on 8 March 2012 is that it was one of five nominees in the 'biggest wave' category in the Billabong XXL Global Big Wave Awards of the same year. What's more, 'Cotty' appears in the same category again – as the jetski driver for Hawaii-based Garrett McNamara, whose ride at Praia do Norte, Nazaré, Portugal on 1 November 2011 has been estimated in many quarters to be in the

90 ft region. With McNamara's Nazaré wave also nominated in what is arguably the most prestigious category, the Ride of the Year, Cotton – a plumber by trade and the vice-chairman of Croyde Surf Club – is realising his dream: to make a mark as an international big wave surfer.

"I've dedicated my life to surfing big waves," says Cotton. "I don't mind if I have to tow into them or paddle into them. I just love big waves, and I want to do something to make my kids and girlfriend proud."

Cotton's determination saw him travel to Ireland and meet up with long-time tow-surfing partner Al Mennie as soon as it became clear that 50 ft waves would be bombarding the west coast towards the end of the first week of March. It was Mennie who introduced Cotton to the Emerald Isle's big wave potential: "I met Al on a surf trip to Madeira a few years ago. We didn't score anything too huge and by the end of the trip Al told me there were bigger waves back in Ireland. Almost as soon as I returned to North Devon the phone went. It was Al telling me that a massive swell would be hitting Donegal Bay. I went over. That was the first time I surfed Mullaghmore Head and Al was right."

Since then, Cotton has returned often to surf Mullaghmore Head and other Irish bombs, but his regular trips across the Celtic Sea are no boardshorts idyll. The evening before the 8 March 2012 session was, in one sense, luxurious – Mennie and Cotton slept in Mennie's van while usually they camped out in a tent on the headland overlooking Mullaghmore's infamous left-hander, buffeted by howling winds and trying in vain to stay warm. On the night of 7 March, cramped in Mennie's van, they were full of nervous tension. "We knew that massive surf was on its way but in Ireland you can never be sure. The weather changes so quickly and the wind can destroy what could have been perfect waves in a matter of minutes. I've spent so many swells camped on that headland, with the wind wailing and not quite in the right direction. I honestly thought that this was going to be another swell like that."

Mennie and Cotton also believed that the optimum time for the next day's surfing would be from noon. "We thought the swell would drop," explains Cotton, "so after watching a few waves at first light we decided to get in the water straightaway."

Remarkably, they weren't the first. Already in the sea was Tom Butler, a young Englishman from Newquay in Cornwall who had been living in Ireland for the past few months. "Tom was frothing to get in," says Cotton. "He didn't wait, just went straight out. A German guy called Sebastian was towing him. Al and I saw him get two waves before we followed."

The quartet weren't favoured by balmy temperatures, still less, sunshine. The sea temperature was around 8 degrees Centigrade that day; the sky was a deep and relentless grey, the kind of grey that only Ireland's Atlantic coast can produce. The wind chill factor was barely combated by 7 mm winter wetsuits, boots, gloves and hoods, but yet more worrisome was the depth of the reef at Mullaghmore Head. Here, a trip over the falls – when a surfer is pitched from the top to the bottom of a wave, as its lip breaks – could be fatal. "You're looking at a long hold-down, certainly," says Mennie, who wore two impact vests for the session, and whose sense of the pleasure of surfing Mullaghmore says it all. "When you've made it to the channel, at the moment the ride is over – that feeling is intense and amazing."

Before Cotton's first wave, it was Mennie who was credited with riding the biggest wave yet at Mullaghmore. On 1 December 2007, he was towed by South African surfer Duncan Scott into a wave of some 55 ft. That day, Mennie and Scott, together with another tow team – British surfer Gabe Davies and Ireland's Richie Fitzgerald – put down a marker when they successfully tackled gargantuan 50 ft waves breaking over Mullaghmore's deep water reef. Mennie got the wave of the day, and the world sat up and took note; it was Cotton's fate to do likewise in March 2012.

"I trust Al completely," says Cotton, who has dreamt of being a professional surfer since the age of 15. "You have to have that kind of relationship with whoever's going to be out there towing you in. You need to be able to rely on them completely. And you also need to be fully committed. I've seen people get into trouble when they're half-hearted, when they get towed onto a wave but then change their mind. You can't do that. You can't decide to jump off. You've got to pull up high and get on with it. If you're going, you really are going; you can't turn back."

Cotton showed precisely this kind of commitment on the wave he caught at six minutes past ten in the morning, having been towed into it by Mennie. "I didn't even look properly," he says. "I just went for it." Cotton was riding a 5 ft 1 inch Gulf Stream tow board shaped by Julian 'Jools' Matthews, a design that he loves. "I worked for Jools at Gulf Stream for 10 years and I love riding his boards because I know how much time and effort he puts into every shape and minor detail. It gives me a lot of confidence."

That confidence was essential given the way that Cotton attacks big waves: he is not a surfer who is content with a fast ride down the line. "I always like to try to get to the bottom of big waves, rather than take a high line – which is what some people do at Mullaghmore. This wave was the same. As soon as I'd let go of the rope, I angled my board to the trough of the wave. There are always loads of lumps and ledges at Mully, which makes it all the more difficult to ride. It's not a clean, smooth wave like Teahupoo; it's not a wave where you can draw nice, elegant lines. But I made it to the bottom and then angled back up the face. Then there was mid-face fade, then a turn, then a bit of spit. I was going so fast that when I felt the spray, as the lip came down behind me, I thought I'd made it. But I hadn't. And that's when everything went white."

Cotton's memory thereafter is confused. "I just don't remember the feeling, thc actual sensation of what happened. Anyone can see on the video footage that I got nailed in the white water but I can't recall what it actually felt like. Strange, really. I know that I came up and took a breath, even as I was getting worked, and then got taken down again. I also have a vague vision of seeing jetskis in the channel, and then being surprised to see them so far away from where I thought they were when I finally surfaced. I think I must have been carried a good 100 metres."

Experienced tow-surfer that he is, Mennie was quickly on the scene. He picked up Cotton and his tow board, offering a classic piece of understatement. "Al got to me on the ski and just said 'That was alright, quite a big one'. But my adrenalin levels were through the roof."

The pair stayed in the water, swapping so that Mennie could surf with Cotton towing him in, before coming to shore for lunch. It was only on land that Cotton realised what he had achieved – thanks, initially, to Twitter. "I couldn't believe it, but by the time I was back on land there were tweets going round saying that I'd just ridden a bomb. Then I saw the video footage. I thought 'Yep, bloody hell, that was a big wave.'"

In the afternoon, Mennie and Cotton took to the waves again. They were joined by other surfers, including Davies and Fitzgerald and another Irish surfer, Ollie O'Flaherty. None of them managed to top Cotton's wave, but they came close: a wave ridden by Davies was considered for nomination, and one ridden by O'Flaherty ultimately joined Cotton's as one of the potential XXL Biggest Waves of 2012.

Cotton and O'Flaherty found themselves in illustrious company. As well as McNamara's Nazaré monster, extraordinary waves ridden at Cow Bombie in Western Australia and Agiti in the Basque Country by Damien Warr and Axi Muniain respectively, were up for consideration. The winners of the Biggest Wave, Ride of the Year and other categories were announced at a star-studded awards ceremony in Anaheim, California on 4 May 2012. McNamara's Nazaré wave duly scooped the Biggest Wave category – and was also ratified by the Guinness Book of Records as the biggest wave yet surfed, at 78 ft – while the Ride of the Year went to Nathan Fletcher for an incredible ride during Teahupoo's infamous Code Red session of 27 August 2011.

For Cotton – who says that "the more you watch Mullaghmore, the scarier it gets" – being nominated was a tremendous achievement, all the more so given the toll on his body exacted by big wave surfing. "I've snapped my knee ligaments twice and bashed up my pelvis," he reveals, with Mullaghmore being the scene of his undoing on at least one occasion. "I was wearing a knee brace but I fell on a wave at Mully and got seriously beaten – so seriously that it ripped the brace off. I couldn't walk properly for days after that wave."

Stoked after his trip to the Billabong XXL awards night, which was funded by his sponsors (Tiki, Analog and The Thatch, the latter being the popular pub at Croyde), Cotton is entitled to feel confident that his dreams were being realised. It had been a hugely significant year for him, what with bagging a nomination in the Biggest Wave category and being the man who towed McNamara to glory. "I'm so proud for my girlfriend Katie and two children, Honey and Ace. I'm hungry for more now. I hope to return to Nazaré, and I hope to surf other massive waves around the world. I'd like to make my family proud."

But if the world of big wave surfing is set to open up for Cotton, surely there is a limit to the size of the waves that can be ridden at Mullaghmore? The Croyde Bay lifeguard – a summertime role he splits with being a plumber – thinks not. "Mullaghmore will hold any size. And the bigger it gets, the better it gets. But make no mistake: it's a savage wave."

As Andrew Cotton knows better than anyone else, it's also a wave where everything can go white in an instant – but where a reputation can be made for life.

PART FOUR

Gonzo Interlude

BEING DAVE RASTOVICH

"You see the world through John Malkovich's eyes, then, after about 15 minutes, you're spit out onto a ditch on the side of the New Jersey turnpike" – John Cusack, playing Craig Schwartz, in *Being John Malkovich.*

Dave Rastovich, 33, is a professional surfer for the Billabong team. He's tanned and tall, lean and languorous, has high cheekbones and long eyelashes. As happens every December, Rasta is at Billabong's house on the North Shore of the Hawaiian island of Oahu. He's there to bag some serious water time at the many breaks along what is known as 'the seven-mile miracle', the series of world-class waves stretching from the hippie town of Haleiwa on the south-west of the North Shore to Sunset Beach towards the north-eastern point.

Rasta is telling me about his activism on behalf of cetaceans. Or rather, he's trying to tell me. The sound of waves detonating on the reef opposite the Billabong house makes it almost impossible to hear a word. No wonder, for we're standing just yards from the most famous surf break in the world, the Banzai Pipeline. And in surf-speak, it's going off. Pulses of clean surf, generated by storms off the coast of Alaska, are surging irresistibly to the beach. Just before they get there, held up by an offshore breeze, they hit a lava reef, which forces them to rise steeply then break in the form of the hallowed cylindrical tube that provides surfing nirvana.

Just a few days earlier, the Billabong Pipeline Masters – the most prestigious surfing contest of all – was won by Australian surfer Kieren Perrow in surf that was even bigger and better. But if the 20 ft waves of the Pipe Masters have dropped, they haven't done so by much. The residue of one of the best swells ever to grace the iconic event is still a proposition.

Rasta declares that the waves we're witnessing at Pipeline are "friendly". To me, they look anything but. They're easily double overhead – which means the height of the wave face is a solid 10 ft and then some – and a mistake on the take-off would mean a pummelling into the reef: Pipeline breaks in about 2 ft of water.

As I watch, marvelling at how good a surfer you'd have to be to describe the waves in the foreground as "friendly", a middle-aged man with a slight paunch, close-cropped hair and a blue rash vest takes off on one of Pipeline's left-handers. He's riding a longboard. He's not the most elegant of surfers – he's neither a Rasta, nor a patch on the crop of hard-charging aerial experts with whom he's sharing the waves at Pipe today – but he makes the drop with a nicely angled take-off and goes on to enjoy what the average surfer would commend as 'a nice ride'.

I file the man away in my mind as The Fat Longboarder. I'm probably being unfair. Sure, he was riding a longboard, but he wasn't especially overweight. But I like the fact that he has a gut, albeit a humble one rather than my own more assertive midriff. I also like the fact that, like me, he's clearly in his 40s, and I especially like the fact that he's surfing Pipeline on a board which is at least 2 ft longer than those usually seen here.

* * *

It's a sunny day in December 2011. I haven't been here on the North Shore for long, and the trip will be a short one. Short, but for the duration of the eight days that I'll be on Oahu, very sweet. All my life I've dreamt of being here, on the paradisiacal Hawaiian island which hosts the seven-mile miracle, a stretch of breaks – the likes of Pipeline, Off the Wall, Sunset Beach, Waimea Bay and Rocky Point – that are basic names in every surfer's lexicon.

I'm staying at the Turtle Bay Resort and to explore the North Shore I hire a bicycle. The going is even, nice and flat, a breeze for anyone. I stop at the Banzai Pipeline – so named in the Sixties because a surfer is said to have seen a sewer pipe being laid underneath the nearby highway, complete with a sign saying 'Danger – Pipeline', and check out the surf. The waves are friendlier than when I met Rasta for the first time, two days ago. I wonder if he'll be at the Billabong house, and wheel my bike across its nicely cut grass, round to the beachfront patio. The sliding doors are open but no one is home, neither Rasta, nor his girlfriend Lauren Hill, nor any of the other surfers staying there. Why would they be? The surf may be heading to the too-friendly, but it's still clean and over head high. Rasta will be in the ocean, doing his thing. And quite a thing it is, too.

Despite his family hailing from Vis, an island between Italy and Croatia which is not renowned for surfing, Rasta has emerged as one of the 21st century's most recognisable and respected surfers. He was born in New Zealand to Dennis and Yvonne, who separated when he was 14. By then, Rasta had lived on Australia's Gold Coast for eight years. After his parents' separation, Rasta would alternate between spending a week with his father, who lived at Surfer's Paradise, and a week with his mother, whose house was at Burleigh Heads. He started surfing aged five, and besides regarding his parents' split as "for the best – they were better off doing this than clinging on to the idea of staying together" – their residences at prime Queensland surf zones only served to foster talent which was apparent almost as soon as he learnt how to stand up on a board.

As a young boy, Rasta bodysurfed initially. He was also immersed in Australia's surf-lifesaving scene, joining his local club and spending hours swimming, learning a variety of water skills and generally imbuing his body with beach fitness alongside his friend Grant Hackett, who would go on to become an Olympic gold medal winner in swimming. Before 1902 it was illegal to enter the ocean during daylight hours in

Australia, but by the Nineties, when Rasta started winning paddleboard races, surf-lifesaving had become a massive part of Australian coastal life. But for all its popularity, there was something about surf-lifesaving that Rasta didn't like, even as a boy.

"There was something almost military about the surf-lifesaving environment," he says. "As a kid I saw the beach as a place of freedom. Exposure to lifeguards and their fanatical training regimes set me thinking, especially because I could see the fun all the surfers were having out there in the line-up. Surfing is also about freedom. I couldn't understand why anyone would want to build walls around it."

By the age of 15, Rasta was the U-15 boys' world junior champion; by then he was also sponsored by Billabong. He competed for a few years, winning some regional events, holding his own against future world champion Mick Fanning and perennial top-placed contenders Joel Parkinson and Taj Burrow, and once placing fifth in a World Championship Tour event at Mundaka. "I got a wildcard for that one," he explains. "Another time, I got through a few heats at a contest at J-Bay." If Rasta seems vague, almost indifferent about his competition results, it's because they mean very little, possibly nothing, to him. "I walked away from the contest scene when I was 20," he says. "I wanted to go and be a yoga teacher. I also looked at people like Gerry Lopez, Tom Curren, Margo Oberg and Jim Banks – all great surfers who seemed to have so much more fun when they stopped competing."

There are very few professional surfers who can elect to walk away from contests and yet still make a living from surfing – especially at so young an age – but Rasta is one of them. Billabong supported his decision, and now, for over a decade, Rasta has been paid simply to be himself. It's a job he works hard at, with plenty of appearances in surf movies (*Slipping Jetstreams, The Free Way, Blue Horizons,* to name but three) and regular appearances in surf magazines, with a feature for the January 2012 issue of *Surfer* seeing him follow an epic swell from Tahiti to Mexico, and then to Alaska. It was billed as 'the most ambitious surf trip ever' with 18,000 miles covered in eight days. However, if this made for an intense, concentrated bout of work, Rasta is capable of immersing himself in longer projects, too: *Minds in the Water,* a 2011 film which follows Rasta as he publicises the plight of cetaceans in

Australia, the Galapagos Islands, Chile and Japan, was five years in the making.

"If you want something in your life that you've never had, you've got to be prepared to do something you've never done," says Rasta, but there is more to his success than inventiveness allied with media savvy. Rasta is also one of the most stylish surfers on the planet, a man capable of riding any kind of board with grace, fluency and poise; the kind of surfer who makes everything look at once beautiful and effortless. He can pull off all the new school tricks, and is comfortable in big waves but on top of that he is articulate, thoughtful and easy on the eye. Rasta, the man with a mix of Croatian ancestry and Scottish genes, is the 21st century's most complete surfer. He's got it all, and then some. And for a major surf brand like Billabong, he's a marketing dream.

"Our life is a creation of our mind," he says.

* * *

I decide to cycle back to the Turtle Bay, stopping at Pipeline again to see if Rasta is around.

I sit on the beach with my bike on the sand behind me, but I can't see him anywhere. The Fat Longboarder is there, right in front of me, once again riding the lefts of Pipeline.

Who is he? I resolve to ask Rasta if he knows him, but later, when we meet again and talk in earnest, the conversation heads away from surfing.

It goes to *The Cove*.

We're sitting at a table in the kitchen of the Billabong house. Rasta has offered me a drink but can't help with my request for a black coffee. He's a vegan and, it seems, eschews even more than fish and meat. I opt for a chai tea, accompanied by a glass of water, and listen as Rasta expounds on cetaceans and his role in *The Cove.*

The film, directed by former National Geographic photographer Louie Psihoyos, bagged 2010's Oscar for Best Documentary Feature, not to mention a swathe of other prestigious awards. It is a stirring indictment of commercial dolphin slaughter carried out each year in a cove near the Japanese town of Taiji in the Wakayama Prefecture. It features Ric O'Barry, as chief protagonist, provocateur and bane of the

Japanese authorities, who first came to fame in the 1960s for capturing and training the five dolphins that were used in the TV series *Flipper*. If O'Barry initially helped to create the dolphin captivity industry, he experienced a profound conversion when Kathy, one of the dolphins, died in his arms (O'Barry is adamant that Kathy committed suicide). Since then he has campaigned indefatigably to end all trade in dolphins, setting about freeing them whenever possible and making as much noise as he can against the leading whaling nations, of which there is really only one – Japan.

Rasta knew a fair bit about Japan before he discovered that an annual dolphin drive led to their mass slaughter by Taiji fishermen in a cove that was not only hidden from public view, but also zealously guarded by both fishermen and public officials. "For some reason, the Japanese loved the whole hippie surfer thing, and I was really popular there from around 2005 to 2007," he tells me. Less than a 100 yards away, amped groms and athletic 20-somethings make Pipeline look like a mellow beachbreak rather than the world's deadliest wave. I find it difficult not to watch – this level of performance surfing is incredible – but Rasta has seen it all before, a hundred times, a thousand times. Besides, the more we talk, the more I get the feeling that even if Pipe was epic, as it was just a week earlier for the Billabong Pipeline Masters, Rasta would still rather talk about cetaceans than stare at waves he wasn't riding.

"There's a big surfing community around Taiji and some great surf," says Rasta. "It was through some local surfers that I learnt about what was happening in Taiji to thousands of dolphins each year. I was shocked, really shocked. One of the places I surfed a lot when I was growing up was Byron Bay, where dolphins are a regular sight. I couldn't believe that fishermen would corral them and then kill so many at once, stabbing them repeatedly with spikes until the sea turns blood red."

But the more Rasta talked to those in the know, the more it seemed that Taiji – ostensibly a small, pleasant coastal town – had a dark and troubling secret. No matter that statues of whales stood proudly in parts of Taiji; no matter that there were murals featuring dolphins here and there, still less that the town's children would happily walk around with cuddly toys of cetaceans: footage taken at the cove by Hardy Jones, an ocean conservationist and co-founder of BlueVoice.org (an organization dedicated to protecting whales and dolphins), revealed the full horror of the Taiji dolphin drives. As soon as he saw the visual evidence, Rasta was determined to do something about it:

"I started to seek out environmentalists who'd been to Taiji, people who knew what was happening there. I talked to Paul Watson, who's been defending and protecting marine wildlife for over 30 years through the Sea Shepherd Conservation Society. I learnt more from Paul and then I met Ric O'Barry and talked to him. I discovered that every breath a dolphin takes is a conscious decision, that it's impossible to anaesthetize them – they're so sensitive. I attended some IWC meetings to try and find out as much as I could about how I could peacefully do something to stop the slaughter. Then Ric told me about the project with Louie Psihoyos – about their plan to go to Taiji and document what was happening there. That's when it came to me: the idea to paddle out into the cove, at the time of the dolphin drives, and peacefully protest about what was going on."

As we're talking Lauren joins us at the table. She is 26, has long blonde hair and degrees in environmental and social science from Stetson University in Florida. She smiles gently and helps herself to some chai. Lauren is also a professional surfer with her speciality being longboarding. As she is on land – supple, charming, balletic – so too is Lauren on a longboard.

Lauren's appearance makes for the antithesis of the images in my mind, conjured both by Rasta's account and my memories of scenes from *The Cove.* Rasta tells me of how he and a small group journeyed to Japan with the idea of forming a surfers' circle in the cove. They would then join hands and, as he puts it, "send love to the dolphins, the ultimate surfers, in a place where there has been so much violence". The idea was good in theory but not so congenial in its execution. The Taiji fishermen got wind of the group's arrival and, if they couldn't be sure of their precise plan, sensed that Rasta and his friends were not in Taiji for surf brand promotional purposes. The first time the group, which included American actress Hayden Panettiere, Australian TV star Isabel Lucas, surfer Vaya Phrachanh and professional mermaid Hannah Fraser arrived at the cove, there was, says Rasta, "a lot of tension. They thought we were going to riot or something. We'd decided to paddle out and form the circle no matter what, but they made it impossible".

But later, the group was able to form the circle. Some 20 individuals paddled their boards into the cove, linked hands and sent their respects to the cetaceans. This they accomplished without any friction, before the mood turned sour again and they had to leave. But still later Rasta received a tip-off: the fishermen had been to sea and captured some 25 pilot whales. They had driven them into the cove and killed them or, in many cases, injured them so grievously that they could go home and simply leave them to die. This time a smaller group, including Panettiere and Lucas, managed to sneak back to the cove and paddle their boards close to the dying whales. This time, things went from sour to downright nasty.

"We managed to create a small circle," says Rasta, "but the fishermen were freaking out. One took his boat ashore and went and got some other fishermen. They came back and brought the boat alongside us. One of them had a boat pole. He started hitting the girls on their legs with it, bashing their boards too. Then the fishermen realised that they were being filmed. They backed off a bit but on land it was really intense. A few of us had breakdowns. It was so sad. I had a knife in my pocket and I wanted to swim over and cut the nets to try and set free the pilot whales that were still alive. But we'd resolved to make sure this was a peaceful protest. Things were getting ugly enough as it was. It was tough to walk away but we had to."

In *The Cove,* one fisherman distinguishes himself by the mix of the ferocity of his language, a habitually demonic facial expression and his predilection for filming those he and his comrades regard as inimical to an ancient Japanese custom. The film crew give him a name which reflects the only two words of English that he ever utters: 'Private Space'.

Private Space can be seen ranting at a cameraman shortly after the second paddle out by Rasta. I recall his extraordinary aggressiveness as Rasta concludes his tale. So too, do I recall the dreadful images of brutal dolphin slaughter in *The Cove*. I feel myself getting angry. It is all so senseless. The captivity industry is surely wrong. Dolphins like Flipper may amuse the crowds, but Rasta avows that they've learnt their tricks because they've been conditioned by starvation and Taiji dolphin drives supply a number of dolphinariums around the world. In addition, dolphin meat isn't even good to eat: at Taiji, residents have dangerously high mercury levels owing to their fondness for cetaceans.

Because cetaceans are at the top of the food chain their mercury levels are high, having accumulated it from all the fish lower in the food chain. As Louis Psihoyos puts it, "If you're eating dolphin meat, you're eating poison, and if you're eating a lot of dolphin meat, you're eating a lot of poison."

Sitting in the Billabong house, listening to Rasta, I feel angry about the Taiji dolphin drives. I'm not sure I'd have covered myself in pacific glory if I'd been one of Rasta's group.

"How did you keep your cool?" I ask.

"I try my best to be a very peaceful person," replies Rasta.

* * *

"Surfing is one of the most beautiful things in the world," says Lauren. "You get to see the amazing in the ordinary. You notice things that you wouldn't otherwise see, like a pair of butterflies in the rainbow of a breaking wave, and you reassess your place in it all, suspended in an environment that's constantly moving and changing."

Lauren has earlier been surfing Chun's Reef, one of the more mellow north shore breaks. She grew up on Florida's Anastasia Island, was the US girls' longboard champion in 2002 and, like Rasta, has walked away from contest surfing to carve out an existence as a free surfer. She rides for Billabong and Bing Surfboards. On the latter's website, Lauren says her favourite move is "just standing there".

Lauren shares Rasta's passion for cetaceans. Shortly before coming to Oahu, she took part in the second voyage to be conducted under the auspices of TransparentSea, a campaign set up to raise awareness of coastal environmental issues. The first journey, along the coast from Byron Bay to Bondi Beach in 2009, highlighted the plight of humpback whales and the threat faced by Japanese whaling fleets, while the second, in October 2011, traced the southern migration of the California grey whale from Santa Barbara to Baja, Mexico. Lauren tells me that she, Rasta and their fellow travellers sailed down the Californian coast in a 16 ft Hobie, sailing the kayaks in exquisite, sunny but largely windless weather. "We had to pedal most of the way," she says, but the effort was worth it for the group's encounters with marine life – not least, on one occasion, some blue whales.

"It was towards the end of the day," says Lauren. "The sun was beginning its descent when we saw a spout of water on the horizon. We started pedalling as fast as we could towards it, thinking we would see some grey whales. But as we got closer we could see that the spouts were 20-30 ft high. Then Howie [Cooke, an artist and cetacean activist] shouted 'They're blue whales! They're definitely blue whales!' I couldn't believe it. We spent two hours with the whales, who were between 80 and 100 ft long. They were incredible. They had no sense of fear, and the amazing thing was that they were making the decision to come and check us out. We could see their tail flukes, and one of the whales rolled on its side as it swam next to Dave's boat. It was beautiful. To think this happened so close to the sprawling humanity of southern California. None of us wanted to leave. It felt like a blessing. And it was all made possible by surfing."

It's getting dark. I've spent a few hours talking to Rasta and Lauren, but now it's time to cycle back along the Kamehameha Highway and return to the Turtle Bay Resort. Before I leave, I ask Rasta about the effect on his career of the incident at the cove.

"Billabong were really supportive," he tells me "but I was blackballed by the Japanese surf media. Posters and films were pulled. I heard through friends that a lot of surf shops were visited by heavies. There's a saying in Japan: 'The nail that sticks out must be slammed back down.' It's true. Japan has such a conformist, historically non-confrontational culture that it's very difficult to make a stand."

But if Rasta's visibility in Japan may have taken a dive, his protest, and *The Cove* itself, have made a difference. The plight of cetaceans is once again at the forefront of many environmental campaign groups, not least that which was co-founded by Rastovich himself: S4C, or Surfers for Cetaceans. Rasta believes that dolphin meat is no longer as popular as it was in Japan pre-*The Cove*, and activists make it their business to be at Taiji every year for the dolphin drives, making it more and more difficult for Japan to defend what its politicians continue to claim is an ancient and venerable custom. Similarly, the captivity industry is under the spotlight. Is it right that dolphins should be captured and sold for between $150,000-200,000 each? Many people are now asking the question, thanks to Rasta, the creators of *The Cove* and the poacher-turned-gamekeeper himself, Ric O'Barry.

I stand up to make my farewells. There's time to ask Rasta one last question. He has various tattoos of whales and dolphins, and on his right foot are the words 'Without love we perish'. But on his left forearm there's a more bellicose image, one that doesn't quite fit. It's of a sword on a shield, against a backdrop of a wave. Why is it there?

"All the men in my family have this," explains Rasta, who lives in New South Wales behind Byron Bay, on a small organic farm with Lauren. "The sword represents strength and direction. The wave signifies Croatia's seafaring culture. If you add the symbolism of the shield, I guess you're looking at the dualistic nature of my life."

* * *

'Rastovich! Rastovich! Rastovich!'

There's a scene in *Being John Malkovich* in which Malkovich, on the trail of the lascivious Maxine (played by Catherine Keener), finds the portal on floor seven and a half of the Mertin Flemmer building and enters it. Thus far, the portal has taken users inside the head of John Malkovich; now John Malkovich is inside his own head. He finds that everyone looks like him and that the only word they can say is 'Malkovich'.

'Malkovich! Malkovich! Malkovich!' says John Malkovich. 'Malkovich! Malkovich! Malkovich!', says everyone in this universe of Malkovichian ubiquity. It is too much for John Malkovich. He is ejected from the portal into the ditch by the side of the New Jersey turnpike. There he meets Craig Schwartz, the puppeteer played by John Cusack who first discovers the portal, and demands that it be shut down. Schwartz refuses.

Back in England my turnpike is Sennen Cove in the far west of Cornwall. As turnpikes go, it's not bad. Hell, Sunny Garcia even has Sennen as his middle name. But I keep thinking of two things – a world in which everyone is Dave Rastovich, and The Fat Longboarder.

On the day of my 46th birthday, a friend calls me to say that Spot G, a secret spot not too far from Sennen, is pumping. I down tools and drive to the cliff-top car park. My friend is right. In my rush to scamper down the 500 or so granite steps to the beach, there's barely time to acknowledge long-time local Jonty Henshall, who's just been surfing, as is Jonty's preference for every single day of his life come what may, but we have a brief chat and then, minutes later, I'm tying my leash and paddling out into the Atlantic. Another friend, Tup, is in the line-up, and there are a couple of guys who we don't know. Under bright late March sunshine Tup and I share waves and have a great session.

In the world of Rastovich, this happens all the time. This, and all that goes with it: the love of marine life, the fidelity to the environment, the kinship with dolphins and whales, the effort to live a good and decent and peaceful existence.

'Rastovich! Rastovich! Rastovich!'

* * *

A few days later I'm watching a video about North Shore local and surfing extrovert Jamie O'Brien. He's shredding Pipeline, as is his wont – O'Brien grew up at Pipe, and won the Pipeline Masters in 2004 before he had even turned 20 – but the film also features a middle-aged man with a slight paunch, close-cropped hair and a blue rash vest. He's not the smoothest surfer, but time and again he is shown taking off on a longboard at sizeable Pipe and having a series of what anyone who surfs would commend as nice, if inelegant, rides.

The man explains that he was formerly a truck driver who made his living on the American mainland, earning 33 cents a mile. He would sleep in the back of his truck and spend his free time reading surfing magazines, dreaming of returning to Hawaii. Now he has realized his dream. O'Brien's voiceover reveals that the man, who is 49, lives in the bushes somewhere on the North Shore. His *raison d'être* is surfing. He lives for riding Pipeline.

The man's name is Albert.

Being Dave Rastovich yields Albert, aka The Fat Longboarder, aka a man who is nearly 50 who refuses to give up his dream, who says: "I like surfing . . . if you don't kill yourself, and if you don't get crazy, you can do it for years to come . . . you shouldn't give up your hobbies and aspirations. This is the life I choose."

Rastovich!

A THRUST TOO FAR

Simon Anderson, the inventor of the thruster, proves to be elusive on Oahu.

The surfers' bar at the Turtle Bay Hotel and Resort is packed. It's 8pm on the evening of Wednesday 14 December 2011, and I'm one of the throng which has gathered to listen to Simon Anderson talk about his biography.

Here on the North Shore of Oahu, it's a safe bet that everyone in the bar is a surfer. The Turtle Bay Resort may have been the backdrop to *Forgetting Sarah Marshall,* a 2008 film notable for one of cinema's most absurd pseudo-surf scenes (Russell Brand, playing rock star Aldous Snow, purportedly learns to surf in a sea which is denuded of even a wisp of white water, let alone a wave), but almost every North Shore après-surf event is held here, and besides, why take yourself along to a talk by one of the icons of surfing if you don't surf?

Anderson's book is called *Thrust: The Simon Anderson Story.* He is appearing in conversation with Jodi Wilmott, an articulate surfer-turned-well-placed PR in Hawaii, and the ambience is expectant. Everyone in the audience owes a debt of gratitude to the man who from the age of

16, made his mark first at North Narrabeen, New South Wales, and then, as a tall, muscular and yet smooth, natural footer, at surf breaks all over the world.

We all owe Anderson because, in 1980, he stuck an extra fin on one of his surfboards. Two years later, shapers everywhere had adopted what Anderson christened the 'thruster'. The skittish twin fin mutated into the thruster; so, too, the stable single fin. The three-fin set-up had a racy name which Sigmund Freud may have enjoyed pondering, had he but been alive to do so, but sexual connotations aside there was no doubting its efficacy. Thanks to the thruster, surfers suddenly had more drive, more control, more *purpose.*

Anderson never sought a patent for the thruster, but had he done so, he would surely have eclipsed even the sums won by his father on the lottery in the late 1950s. His father's good fortune had a dramatic effect on the Anderson family. They moved from the Sydney suburb of Balgowlah to a beach-front house at Collaroy, near Narrabeen. Simon's older brother, Mark, swam for Australia in the 1968 Olympics. Swimming was also Simon's forte, but his birthday present when he turned 13 – a surfboard – pushed him in a different direction. Four years later, having immersed himself in surfing and mastered the famous left-handers of North Narrabeen (a proving ground that gave him exceptional ability on his backhand), Anderson became the Australian junior champion. He repeated the feat the following year in 1972, and went on to finish third in the world tour in 1977.

Later, in 1981, and armed with his pioneering thruster, Anderson won back-to-back victories at the Bells Beach Classic and the Coke Surfabout in Sydney (events which he had previously won on a single fin), before taking the spoils at that year's Pipeline Masters. The surf world was agog. What was this new design, and how had it come about?

At around the time Anderson was revolutionising surfboard design and cementing his reputation in the sport forever, I was 15 and far more interested in football than anything else. Stan Bowles, the maverick striker who played for Queens Park Rangers, was my hero. I spent hours trying to emulate his tricks, dreaming of making it as a pro footballer, but living by the sea in Devon, I also spent a fair bit of time windsurfing, rowing and swimming. Surfable waves were rare in my part of the world, but a couple of years later one of my closest friends persuaded a group of us that we should drive to Saunton in north Devon and try surfing. I didn't give up my dreams of playing for QPR – in fact, they only faded in my 40s, a confession which makes me either very sad or absurdly optimistic – but I was hooked by surfing. From then on, it became as big a motivating force in my life as football.

But I've never been one for the intricacies of design. Maybe this is because I'm not a practical man. Maybe it's because I lack the requisite attention to detail. Whatever: my view, of surfboards, cars, bikes and all the rest of the paraphernalia with which we surround ourselves, and without which we seem unable to live our lives, is that if they work, great. If they don't, move on.

My lack of interest in design means that I've never been big on fin set-ups, debates about volume, the width of rails, the depth of channels and all the rest of it. But even someone like me appreciates what Anderson did for surfing when, in October 1980, he observed a small half-moon fin nestling between the twin fin set-up of another Narrabeen surfer, Frank Williams. Anderson asked him what the third fin was for, to which Williams replied that it was "a trigger point", something that made his board more stable. At once, inspiration struck. Anderson had been unsuccessful in small surf on the world tour, as much because of his twin fin's inherent instability as his size (Anderson is 6 ft 3inches tall). He decided there and then to add a third fin to the board, but, unlike the one he'd seen on Williams' board, he made it the same size as its outriders. The thruster was born. It worked at once, connecting through turns perfectly and providing drive and stability.

At the Turtle Bay surfers' bar Anderson is laconic as he answers Wilmott's questions. She bills him as "a gentle giant" who "knocked gently while others busted down the door", a reference to a group of young Australian and South African surfers who blitzed the North Shore in the 1970s. Among their number was four-times world champion Mark Richards and 1977 champion Shaun Tomson. Rougher edges were evident in men like Wayne 'Rabbit' Bartholomew, Ian Cairns and Peter Townend (known as PT), whose bravado as they took on local Hawaiian surfers (characterised as "stagnating" by Rabbit in a notorious article entitled 'Bustin' Down the Door'), ultimately led to violence and death threats. Anderson though, evaded any such controversy, perhaps because of his down-to-earth, bloke-next-door persona. As the surf journalist Phil Jarratt once put it, Anderson "likes his snooker, the pub and his mates, and can watch television for three or four days at a stretch". Moreover, wrote Jarratt, he never deviated from "the pursuit of ordinariness".

In the dimmed lights of the surfers' bar Anderson certainly seems intent on ordinariness. Sprawling on a chair that looks too small (but then, most chairs would look too small for such a large man), he makes for a determinedly casual, unstudied counter to his elegantly attired interviewer. He speaks in an unremarkable monotone and is by turns self-deprecating and acerbic. Writing *Thrust* was, he admits, "cathartic", but then he says he doesn't know what the word means. Of the great South African surfer Shaun Tomson, Anderson says "I was never afraid of Shaun. Whenever I'd see him walking across rocks he was kind of effeminate. It was quite a sight." He also wryly notes that he was "privileged to help PT to one of the many second places in his career".

Of the infamous thruster, he says "It was a Narrabeen thing. Twin fins were too loose. They had a tendency to spin out. Single fins were too static. The thruster was the answer, but if I hadn't done it, someone else would have done. I was just lucky that I came up with it and made sure that you all got to know about it."

After winning the Pipeline Masters using a thruster, Anderson was set fair with his invention. The event was "the final frontier", he tells Wilmott, and the proof was in the pudding: since 1984 every world champion has ridden a thruster. Anderson began to market thrusters with Energy Surfboards, who enjoyed a competitive advantage for a short time. Soon though, the design had been copied by just about every surfboard manufacturer in the world. What then of Anderson's failure to patent it?

I recall a line from pre-eminent surf writer Matt Warshaw's *Encyclopedia of Surfing* to the effect that in later life, Anderson "joked somewhat bitterly" about his failure to obtain a patent, "thus missing out on perhaps millions of dollars in licensing fees". The issue crops up in conversation with Wilmott, but Anderson professes equanimity: "Design wisdom can't flourish if someone tries to 'own' an idea," he says.

He's right of course, and while I've wondered at some of Anderson's barbs, now I'm impressed. It's one thing for intellectual property lawyers to regurgitate the legal principle that an idea cannot be owned, but it's another to see one's idea adopted by the world with a fraction of the financial return that would have been possible, if one had but reduced it to material form (thus garnering the protection of copyright law), or more accurately in Anderson's case, secured a patent. But Anderson is sanguine. He shrugs his broad shoulders and Wilmott moves on.

A waitress scurries around serving beers to the crowd as the conversation ambles to its end. There are whoops as slides reveal local hero Bobby Owens in competition against Anderson at massive Bell's Beach in 1981, an event that pitted single fin versus thruster – and saw the thruster prevail.

It's been an entertaining evening. Wilmott wraps things up and the crowd applauds Anderson. Copies of *Thrust* are for sale. I join the queue. When I reach Anderson, I chance the revelation that I'm a writer. I wonder if Anderson would like to talk some more, about the thruster, about his life, anything he likes really, to contribute to a collection of surf stories that I'm working on called *Amazing Surfing Stories*. "Your story would be great," I say, "and I'd be sure to mention your book."

Anderson is nonplussed. He stands tall, towering over me, arms folded, brow furrowed and eyes radiating suspicion. He mutters something about "talking to Jodi". It is clear that our short and not so sweet conversation is over, and that there will not be another one. I slink away, off into the shadows.

It's a shame. Like all surfers the world over, I'm in debt to Anderson. I just wanted to say 'thanks, mate'. But maybe Anderson felt that the cathartic process with which he had so recently engaged was about to be hi-jacked; maybe, having failed to patent the thruster, this possibility was too much to bear. Who knows? My intentions were honourable, so all it remains to say is: thanks, Simon.

DO YOU KNOW RUSSELL WINTER?

Sometimes, the world of surfing is not all that it seems.

Mundaka, northern Spain, autumn 2006. It's the Billabong Pro, one of the top events of the World Championship Tour (WCT). The best professional surfers on the planet have descended on a Basque country village that would tend to the somnolent were it not for the extraordinary river-mouth left-hander on its doorstep.

I'm excited to be in Mundaka, an understated place whose wave is the stuff of legend – not least because it disappeared the preceding year. A little way up the Ria de Mundaka is a government-funded shipbuilding concern, which produces a ship once every five years. In 2005, Mundaka's river-mouth had to be dredged so that the most recently completed ship could make its way to the ocean. The dredging displaced the sandbanks which create Mundaka's tubular paradise, causing the wave to vanish.

Not for long, though. Rumours of the death of Mundaka as a surf break proved to be exaggerated. The seabed contours reformed and the wave was back in time for local heroes like Guillermo Lekunberri to fall in love with it afresh, and declare, mindful of its fragility in the face of commercial imperatives: "We have a proud tradition of surfing in Mundaka, and we must do everything that we can to protect this wave. It is too beautiful too lose."

It also returned in good time for the Billabong Pro, save for one problem – sandbanks will only produce world-class waves if there is swell. The day I arrive at Mundaka there isn't even a hint of swell. The contest organisers have no option but to call a lay day. And worryingly, a glance at the charts reveals that this might well turn out to be a lay week.

So, on a grey and nondescript afternoon, I pad around Mundaka, hoping against hope for some action. Surfing action, that is. Within a short time I'm hearing talk of other kinds of action – one well-known surfer is described as "a man-slut", a soubriquet bestowed because, in less than 24 hours, he has apparently already slept with three local women, while a wiry, fast-talking man with no hair is keen to sell me "anything" I'd like – "uppers, downers, coke, speed, weed – you name it, bro". I wonder if he could get me a copy of *The Times*, but decide against asking, and continue to amble around Mundaka. However, there is nothing to do. The bars are shut, the cafés are closed. No one is about. It must be siesta time.

The crème de la crème of world surfing must be in hiding. Usually, in surf towns which are playing host to surf contests, you can find surfers at every turn. Their uniforms give them away, and they pay no regard to quaint traditions like the Spanish siesta. This afternoon, though, I can't find a single one.

This is frustrating. I'm here to write about the miracle of Mundaka's return as a surf break for a British newspaper, and to interview Mark Occhilupo, the great Australian surfer, for *Huck* magazine. Occy is nowhere to be seen, and there's no one to talk to about the wave. I return to my apartment – for yes, I am lucky enough to have been given an apartment for the duration of my stay – and do some work. I wonder whether to go and buy some beers, but decide against it. After all, I have a job to do. I do some more work. I turn on the TV and watch the Spanish news. It is incomprehensible to me, impoverished a linguist as I am. I receive a text message. It's from the PR, and is in English. She invites me to a restaurant in the centre of Mundaka for an early evening meal. "Great," I say, "where is it?" She replies "It's not difficult to find. See you later."

There are still a few hours to kill. I go for another walk. The scenery is fine. Mundaka overlooks the tidal estuary at the heart of the Urdaibal Biosphere Reserve. Lush hills, many covered in Cantabrian holm oak, sweep down to the Mundaka estuary, itself a major stopover on the migratory route of aquatic birds such as spoonbill as well as home to year-round residents – sandpipers, osprey, terns, kingfishers and herons. About a mile offshore, smack in the impact zone of the huge swells that dominate this part of the Bay of Biscay, is the tiny island of Izaro, used by Sir Francis Drake in the 16th century, both as a base from which to attack passing vessels and as a hiding place for stolen treasure. Apparently, monks used to row out to Izaro for its solitude. Now, Mundaka and its two neighbouring villages hold annual rowing races to Izaro. The winner gets to plant its flags and owns the island for a year.

I find the restaurant and meet the PR. She's bright and blonde and she's called Posy. I've never met anyone called Posy before. I tell Posy the story of Izaro. She's interested, and so are one or two of her colleagues, but her attention – and that of the other journos and PR people on our table – is distracted by the arrival of a superstar. Kelly Slater slinks smoothly past, to take a seat at the table behind us. He's all feline grace and poise, lithe and languorous, a leopard among little people. The girls love him. The men are captivated, too. Izaro and its monks lose their appeal.

Taj Burrow is sitting near me. The man from Yallingup, Western Australia finished second on the 1999 World Tour, and is down to earth and friendly. He talks about property investment rather than surfing, which proves to be about as far as possible from the dialogue I encounter with another top surfer in Mundaka's main bar after supper.

Posy introduces me to Bruce Irons, the brother of Andy, then a three-times world champion. I know Bruce to be an incredible surfer, likewise the man standing next to him in the bar – a rehabilitated Occy. Mark Occhilupo, a Sydney-born goofy-footer, started setting the WCT ablaze aged 17, having blitzed a number of Australian amateur events. In the blink of a trademark snap, Occy was dominating the top five and, with Tom Curren, was set for iconic status way before he could handle it. The pressure finally got to the 5 ft 9 inch powerhouse – once dubbed 'The Raging Bull' – and by the late 1980s what the surfing world knew of Occy was merely a memory. His weight ballooned, there were rumours of drink and drugs, and anyone who'd predicted that Occy would get his act together, go running every day for six months and return to pro surfing would have been laughed off the beach. That, however, is just what he did – and then some. In 1999, at the inaugural Billabong Mundaka Pro, Occy slotted in to a tube that was as long and hollow as anything that the Basque country's premier wave has ever delivered. Cue a perfect 10, and a ride that is still talked about in awe. Occy went on to win the event and with it, the World Title at the age of 33.

But tonight, Occy is not on form. Posy and I are with a South African woman who's helping out with PR. She is beautiful. Bruce is obviously taken with her. Occy, though, is speechless. He manages to shake hands as we're introduced, and mumbles what might be agreement when I say that I look forward to talking to him the following day. But then he stands uneasily still and enacts a bizarre ritual, first putting a hand down the front of his trousers and having a fulsome scratch, then doing the same but this time with his backside the focus of his attention. He does this again and again. At no stage is a hand not fiddling with his nether regions. I catch the South African's eye. She raises her eyebrows. It is clear that neither of us has ever met anyone who engages in genital rearrangement quite so publicly.

Bruce, though, is oblivious. He seems delighted by the news that I live in England. "Hey, so you're from England! That's awesome bro!" He asks if I live in Newquay. I say no, but I know the place well. Bruce likes this too, and then an idea occurs.

"Do you know Russell Winter?"

I reply that I do. This is not strictly true.

"Hey! That's awesome bro! I know Russ!"

I smile and think that I should explain that actually, I don't know Britain's most successful surfer very well. In fact, despite meeting him on numerous occasions, and even once turning up at his house in

Newquay, the timing has never been right for an interview that I'd love to do. After all, Winter has beaten Kelly Slater (in an event at Sunset Beach, Oahu) and made it onto the WCT, only to suffer an injury at Teahupoo that disrupted his career. He's known and respected by the global surfing elite as a brilliant, aggressive surfer in any conditions. He's a charger. But he's also notoriously elusive when it comes to the media. Whenever I see him, he smiles and says yes, of course, let's sit down and talk, and yet it never happens. My experience as a writer wishing to profile Britain's best ever surfer is far from unique. Winter is sought here and he is sought there; rarely, in a media-friendly way, is he to be found.

I refrain from saying all this to Bruce. In any event, before I can say anything, he's off again.

"Hey bro," he says, leaning towards me. This is unfortunate, for Bruce has evidently vomited a little earlier. His breath reeks.

"Yes?" I say.

"Do you know Russell Winter?"

I wonder if Bruce is taking the mick. I say "Er, yes, I do."

"That's awesome bro!" exclaims Bruce, standing back. Then, after a pause, he leans towards me again. I think I know what he's going to say.

"Hey bro . . . do you know Russell Winter?"

This goes on for a few more minutes. Bruce is drunk. I know this because it's obvious, and because I have wrestled with serious drinking at times in my life, always coming off worse. Bruce is locked into the syndrome of being sufficiently drunk as to not be able to remember what he has just said. All the while, Occy scratches his genitals, saying nothing. I disengage – somehow – and go outside for some fresh air. A wiry bald-headed man is there, leaning against a wall. He fires questions at me, eyes ablaze and intense. "Hey man, want some speed? Some coke? Some weed? I got whatever you want. Come on, man, it's party time!" I decline, politely saying that drugs aren't my thing but that I wouldn't mind a copy of the day's *Times*. He stares at me as if I'm an alien.

The following day I am supposed to meet Occy at 10am. He fails to show. I'm told he'll be with me at 11. It's another no show. The no shows go on all day, but eventually we meet at 6pm. There is now a tiny wave at Mundaka, but it's not big enough to host the contest. But however lacklustre the surf, it is nothing compared with the lifelessness of my conversation with Occy. It's not even desultory. He can barely string a sentence together. His hangover is a thing of terrible grandeur. It's easily the worst interview of my career.

Six years later, Andy Irons tragically died in a Texas hotel room. Initially it was claimed that dengue fever was the cause of death, but belatedly what everyone in surfing knew was accepted – that a misuse of various drugs was responsible. *The Times* asked me to write Irons' obituary, which I duly did, *sans* reference to what everyone knew, for in professional surfing no one talks about drugs – they're not the kind of action the sponsors want; they don't sit well with the sport's clean-cut image.

But later, in early 2012, the Association of Surfing Professionals (surfing's international governing body) announced that dope testing would be introduced for pro surfing contests. A new ASP Anti-Doping Policy would apply to all the top 34 men and the top 17 women competing on their respective ASP World Title series, a development which Kieren Perrow, an ASP Top 34 competitor and the surfers' representative, described as "a positive step which enhances the professionalism of competitive surfing and sends a great message to the kids out there who look up to us as role models."

Meanwhile, I look back on years of writing about surfing and recall that even when I spent two weeks in an apartment on Barbados beneath one in which Russell Winter was staying, I still didn't manage to pin him down. So, the truthful answer to Bruce Irons' question – "Do you know Russell Winter?" – is no, not really, I know who he is and recall watching him score a perfect 10 with one of the best tube rides I've ever seen at the O'Neill Highland Open in Scotland and we've had a few brief chats here and there, but I can't say I know him properly, I can't say yes, I know Russell Winter, but, I can say, Bruce, that he's a damn fine surfer, as you are too, though if you don't mind me asking, why have you taken to surfing Teahupoo wearing a blindfold?

FOUR SURFERS AND A PAINTING

A strange journey starts at a service station and ends up in Hawaii.

Once there was a painting. It was made by Tony Plant, a tall man from Newquay who rarely wears shoes. Tony is a surfer, surf photographer, artist and enthusiast. Nothing in life seems to get him down. He always sees the best in people, always has something positive to say. He never moans and his love of the ocean is as palpable as a 40 ft wave.

The painting created by Tony was of the last tree on earth. It was inspired by a surf trip in 2011 to the Mentawai Islands with a group of British surfers: Russell Winter, Nigel Semmens, Spencer Hargreaves, Timmy Boydell, Taz Knight and Tom Good.

After a day in the water with his camera, Tony would jump off the boat used by the crew and paddle ashore. He would then paint. In Tony's case, that means actually painting shells, rocks, stones – the shoreline and its elements. This he would do using bio-degradeable paint to create art of complete evanescence: art which disappears with the outgoing tide. He did this along the chain of islands, and each time brought a selection of damaged wood back onboard. Why damaged? Because the Japanese tsunami had only recently been in the area, wreaking havoc. Numerous islands were smashed, coral heads strewn, trees snapped; the wood Tony was hauling back to the boat was tsunami-damaged wood.

Tony brought some of the wood all the way back to the UK. Back in his hometown of Newquay he started pondering the tsunami-ravaged landscapes that he'd seen. As he put it "The single most striking images that burnt into my head were the surviving trees, often emphasised by the spaces left behind by the vanished trees, those which used to be there. It seemed to me that as well as being indicators of what had happened, they were witnesses too, a measure or a gauge."

Tony then conceived a series of paintings themed along the idea of 'the last tree on earth'. What would it mean to be confronted by this tree? How would viewers respond? Would the response be universal? Would it prompt deep and primeval emotions, if represented in a series of artworks?

Moreover, what if the paintings went on a journey, just as Tony did, as the wood he collected did, as surfers all around the world do all the time, whether riding a single pulse of energy during a daily surf or travelling the world in search of surfing nirvana?

One day Tony rang me to tell me about the 'last tree' paintings. Unbeknown to Tony, I was going to Hawaii a couple of days later. I told him this, one thing led to another, and before I left England we met at Chiverton Cross service station in Cornwall.

Tony was happy. With a broad smile he gave me a painting. I couldn't see what it looked like – it was hidden under layers of bubble-wrap – but Tony's smile turned to a laugh. "I can't believe it!" he exclaimed, "To think that you're going to take it all the way to the North Shore!"

I stowed the painting in my luggage bag, put the bag on the back seat of my car and said farewell to Tony.

The following day I was at Heathrow. Bad traffic *en route* meant that I only just made the flight – as the last person to board. Roughly 24 hours later I was in a taxi, my bags in the boot, being driven from Honolulu airport to the Turtle Bay Hotel at Kuilima Point on the North Shore of Oahu.

It was my first trip to the fabled North Shore. When I awoke I looked out of my hotel window to see lines of head-high waves breaking on Kuilima Point. The first thing I did was go for a surf. The second was to unpack Tony's painting and leave it with Abigail Cruz, who worked at the Hans Hedemann surf school at the Turtle Bay. Later, having spent the morning thinking about it, Abigail said the last tree painting – which, as I discovered, was more of a sketch than the finished article – "evoked a lot of feelings. I'm a country girl and I've always been surrounded by trees. I can't imagine a world without trees. If there was only one left, I'd want to help it stay alive."

Abigail wasn't a surfer, but the next man to contemplate the last tree was – and a very fine one, too. Dave Rastovich, Billabong rider extraordinaire, vegan and campaigner for cetaceans, nodded as I explained the provenance of Tony's painting and then, standing on the decking of the Billabong house opposite Pipeline, took it from me and said "That's cool. Hey painting, say hi to Pipe! Say hi to Off the Wall!"

It felt as if the last tree had been baptised. I could picture Tony grinning at the thought that the painting had travelled from Newquay to Chiverton Cross and now, via American Airlines, to Oahu's North Shore, and to the most famous surf break on the planet. Hans Hedemann chuckled too when he heard of the last tree's journey. But if the man who was once ranked number four in the world was tickled by the painting's odyssey, he was also impressed by the idea animating the series. After gazing at the painting for a few minutes, Hans, who now runs surf schools at Turtle Bay and Waikiki, said: "If this is the last tree on earth, then this tree must last forever. It'll be the beginning of more. All it takes is one."

Similar sentiments were uttered by Buttons Kaluhiokalani, whom I met a couple of days later at Ted's Bakery, a hamburger joint on the north shore which is almost as iconic as the surf breaks a stone's throw away. Buttons is one of surfing's living legends, not least because, as he told me, he has been clinically dead twice. On the first occasion, when he was 38, he was DOA after partying just a little too hard in Waikiki. He came round in hospital when his sister started tickling his feet. Two weeks later, he did the same thing again. This time, à la *Pulp Fiction*, a syringe full of adrenalin stuck into his chest brought him back.

Being dead a couple of times is on the gnarly side of things. But Buttons – a progressive surfer who was way ahead of his time – was locked into the party scene. It took meeting his Tahitian wife, Hiriata, for things to turn round. They met when Buttons was in his mid-forties, and now have a son, Nuutea, and a baby daughter, Nawaiomalukea. In total, Buttons has eight children and eight grand-children. Nuutea and Nawaiomalukea light up his life today; all his children surf.

When he fell for Hiriata, Buttons got his life together. She played a huge part in his rehabilitation and, as he told me, "Hiriata said that if I wanted to be with her, I had to have a plan. So I came up with one – to run my own surf school." That surf school has gone from strength to strength, and Buttons doesn't plan to return to his old ways.

"People still offer me stuff but I always say no. I don't say 'No thank you', because why should I thank them? I just say I don't do that stuff anymore. In that world people are always looking to see you take a fall, to bring you down. I don't thank them; I just say no."

Today he is full of charisma, lean and fit thanks to surfing and a daily 40-minute home gym routine, and big on the aloha spirit. "It's about giving and sharing. It's the way I was raised. It's the Hawaiian way. If you give love, you get love back. If people come here to surf and remember that, they'll be fine."

As for Tony's last tree, he had this to say: "If that's the last tree on earth I'd feel very sad – but I'd get some seeds to plant some more. I'd plant them around the world. I'd tell everyone around the world to plant more seeds. We need more trees."

Sweet and simple, but over on the Big Island, another world class surfer had perhaps the most eloquent response to the painting. On the veranda outside his house (itself set in 11 acres of Ohia forest), still, calm and denuded of anything resembling surfing memorabilia, Shane Dorian listened intently as I narrated the last tree's story. Then he said: "Wait a minute. I'll show you something."

Shane returned with a copy of *The Giving Tree* by Shel Silverstein. First published in 1964, the book is a children's fable. Shane reads it to his son Jackson and daughter Charlie. "It's the saddest story on earth," he told me.

Once there was a tree. So begins Silverstein's story. The tree loved a little boy, who would play on her branches and sleep in her shade. As he grew older, the boy's needs changed. First the tree gave him her apples, so that he could sell them; then she gave him her branches, so that he could make a house; then she gave him her trunk, so that, as a tired and sad old man, he could travel to a new place.

At the end of his life, the boy returns to the tree of his childhood. Now the tree, used up by the boy, is just a stump. The tree says: *I am sorry. I wish that I could give you something but I have nothing left. I am just an old stump. I am sorry . . .* The boy replies: *I don't need very much now, just a quiet place to sit and rest. I am very tired.*

In that case, says the tree, *an old stump is good for sitting and resting. Come, Boy, sit down and rest.*

The tree is happy.

Tony's painting made it back to England; it hangs on a wall in my house and makes me happy too.

PART FIVE

Contests and Communities

HIGHER THAN A HIGH FIVE

At the Pipeline Masters in 1995, two surfers transcended their sport – and surfing transcended itself.

Ever since it was first held in 1971, the Pipeline Masters – which takes place each December at the Banzai Pipeline on the North Shore of the Hawaiian island of Oahu – has been surfing's premier event. Surfers covet victory in the contest, crowds pack the beach from dawn to dusk, and wannabes and hangers-on are as legion as gurus and surfing savants. Their view of the action is the best in professional surfing, with Pipeline's reef set-ups just yards away. Add the winter timing of the contest, when Hawaii is buffeted by massive swells which originate thousands of miles away off the coast of Alaska, and it's no surprise that even the mainstream media, often indifferent when it comes to professional surfing, usually finds space for coverage.

Back in 1971, the winner of the inaugural Pipeline Masters was Jeff Hakman, a man who went on to seek highs from drugs as much as he did from waves. After a career as a pro surfer (at a time when the notion of 'professional surfing' was barely credible), Hakman launched Quiksilver in the United States. Later, he took the brand to Europe. Pretty much all the while, Hakman indulged in various illicit substances, especially heroin. He was in such thrall that he sold his stake in Quiksilver America to fund his habit. Finally, in the late 80s, his friends got him to rehab and he now lives peaceably on the island of Kauai.

In his heyday, Hakman was known as 'Mr Sunset', in acknowledgement of his prowess at the North Shore break, just a couple of miles along the coast from Pipeline. Another surfer of his era was christened 'Mr Pipeline'. Step forward, Gerry Lopez, the winner in 1972 and 1973 of what would become unquestionably surfing's most iconic competition.

Lopez redefined surfing with an exquisitely smooth, effortless style and an immaculate understanding of tube riding. He was so natural and so graceful, that it seemed as if he had been born for nothing else. The roll-call of subsequent Pipe Masters' winners rings loud with other surfers whose talent seemed similarly God-given, including four-time world champion Mark Richards, fellow Australian power surfers Mark Occhilupo and Gary Elkerton; Hawaiian legend Derek Ho, South Africa's Shaun Tomson and the Irons brothers, Andy and Bruce.

Moreover, the Pipe Masters rarely lacks drama. There are innumerable tales of awesome barrels and near-fatal wipe-outs, and as recently as 2011, some of most epic conditions seen in years transpired, with 20-25 ft waves capturing the imagination of the surfing world. After a few days of intense and blistering competition, yet another Australian, Kieren Perrow, took the spoils in a triumph as popular as it was unexpected. But if the likeable Perrow – who doubles as the surfers' representative on the world tour – would have been elated by his win, the chances are that he would point to 1995 as the year in which the Pipeline Masters reached its zenith. For it was then, at the semi-final stage, that surfing transcended itself. Indeed, it was then that surfing transcended sport and became something else entirely.

One sunny day, two men paddled out to do battle in a showdown that could have given either of them not merely the title of Pipeline Master, but also the 1995 world championship. In a red rash vest and white boardshorts was the Floridian phenomenon and preceding year's winner, Kelly Slater. In dark vest and shorts was Rob Machado, Slater's friend and fellow band member (in the nineties the pair played with pro surfer Peter King, in a band called, predictably enough, The Surfers). The surf was not, as in 2011, gargantuan, but it was comfortably in the double-overhead range. That meant that there were barrels to be had, both going left for 'classic' Pipeline or right for Backdoor Pipe. The crowd knew this, and there was a palpable sense of expectation as Slater and Machado entered the sea. What no one knew was quite how many barrels would be had – and quite what would come of the friends being pitted against each other in a make or break contest.

First on the score-sheet was Slater. The natural footer took off on a left-hander and, grabbing a rail, was instantly deep inside the curl of a fast, reeling wall of water, emerging from the tube to perform a rail-to-rail cutback and off-the-top which scored 9.67 (out of a possible 10), albeit that he fell at the end of the ride. Then came another strong ride, this time a brief stand-up barrel at Backdoor which the judges deemed worthy of a 7.50.

Already then, it seemed that Slater was set to dominate, but Machado had other ideas. A goofy-footer, Pipeline was naturally congenial for the Sydney-born surfer, and his first wave was incredible – a ride of speed and style whose entirety was spent in the tube. The judges had no option – this was a perfect 10.

But so was Slater's next wave. Going right at Backdoor once again, he was barrelled for what seemed an age (but was, of course, a matter of seconds). Slater was on fire – and his reaction, a clenched fist which he punched in the air, while looking to the spectators – showed it. Cue another 10, but amazingly, there was more to come. It was another right-hander, and if previously he'd seemed to be in the tube for an age, this time it seemed to be forever. The crowd couldn't believe their eyes – how could any surfer, even one as formidably brilliant as Slater – come out of this wave? But Slater did, perfectly, beautifully, this time throwing his head back to look to the heavens as if in thanks. Yes, it was another perfect 10.

The two surfers were clearly talking to each other in the sea. There was nothing unusual about this – it happens among pro surfers in contests the world over – but after the event Slater revealed that he'd actually let Machado have a wave, even though he wasn't in pole position. "It was serious," he said. "But we got so many good waves, so quick, that it just pushed the competitive thing aside. We were just laughing. A perfect wave came in and I had priority, but I just said 'You want this one?' He goes 'You serious?' and I'm like 'Go, dude! Go! No problem'."

Onlookers sensed that there was something different about what was unfolding. The beach was buzzing as rides of exceptional skill just kept happening. And then came the moment that took the Pipeline Masters 1995 into an uncharted realm. Machado took off on a left-hander and found himself in a stand up barrel every bit as dramatic as the Backdoor rights ridden by Slater. But as he raced out of it, there was Slater, sitting on his board a little way down the line, watching and appreciating every moment. Machado saw his friend, angled his board to carve around him – and, skimming the surface of the sea, put out his left hand. At the same time, Slater instinctively did likewise. The pair high fived in the middle of the biggest surf contest in the world, as if they were two groms who were stoked to have ridden the first unbroken waves of their life. The roar of the crowd could be heard for miles.

History records that Machado scored an 8.67 for this ride and he bagged another 8.67. Slater – just for good measure – then scored a 9.70 for pig-dogging a left-hander that many observers believed should have been awarded yet another perfect 10. To have a chance of winning the world title, Machado had to finish third or higher in the Pipeline Masters and he did just that. If he were to win the title, Slater had to win the whole thing: he went on to defeat Occhilupo in the final and win the second of what are now 11 world titles.

So much for the statistics; what really happened at the 1995 Pipeline Masters was something that defies mathematical – or perhaps any other – explanation. Slater and Machado seized a moment and in so doing they epitomised the unquenchable *joie de vivre* of surfing in circumstances that, for all the balmy breezes and blue skies, could have easily been so very different.

They took a contest, and in that instinctual high five, turned it into a community.

BLACK CLOUDS AND BELLYBOARDS

At the World Bellyboarding Championships 2011, Gwynedd Haslock summed up the spirit of surfing.

The rain is pouring at Chapel Porth beach near the Cornish surfing village of St Agnes, on the morning of the first Sunday of September in 2011. At the edge of the small car park, near a stall selling wooden bellyboards, a woman sits stoically underneath an umbrella. She is in her sixties, but in this, and the purpose of her visit to Chapel Porth, she is far from alone. Welcome to the World Bellyboarding Championships, where the average age of the competitors is middle-aged and upwards.

Gwynedd Haslock has travelled from Playing Place, a village near Truro, to enter the event. She is undeterred by the inclement weather or the surf, which is onshore, lumpy and uninviting. She does though, baulk at the suggestion of entering the sea for the 'expression session', a free-for-all in which men and women ride their bellyboards in any way they please, *sans* the scrutiny of the judges.

"I don't think I'll bother with the expression session," says Gwynedd. "I think I'll keep warm for the main event."

In the car park and at the top of the beach people mill about, sipping cups of tea and making a virtue of the darkening sky. The retro vibe is everywhere, with competitors sporting swimsuits from yesteryear and amiably discoursing on sartorial choices, not to mention provenance. Cannes-based American entrant Scott Bell proudly declares that his costume is a 1934 Jantzen all-in-one with a 'modesty flap', while 23-year-old James Booth, who works at Newquay's Revolver surf shop, sports a one-piece, dark blue and white hooped piece of knitwear that he would be brave to wear in any other environment.

In all, there are some 300 competitors for the Championships, which was the brainchild of local surfers Chris Ryan, a Chapel Porth car park attendant, and Martin Ward, an RNLI lifeguard supervisor. They set up the event, first held in 2002, in honour of the late Arthur Traveller, a Londoner who had come down to the beach every year with his wooden board. The competition has gone from strength to strength, with the numbers of entrants and journalists rising year after year. This time, there's even a film crew from ITV recording a documentary about this eccentric oceanic enterprise.

Gwynedd is unmoved by the media buzz. She waits contentedly under her umbrella, hoping, as does everyone else, that the rain might relent. But if many of the competitors are also hoping for a change in the sea conditions, Gwynedd is too experienced for this. She knows that the prevailing wind and fair-sized swell will make for a day-long onshore mess. She knows this because she has spent a lifetime surfing the Atlantic waves of Cornwall.

Gwynedd was the British, English and Cornish women's champion on many occasions between 1967 and 1976. She represented Britain in the European Championships at Seignosse, France in 1975, and in June 1978 attended Buckingham Palace by invitation of HRH the Prince of Wales, who was then the patron of the now defunct British Surfing Association. The Prince had expressed a wish to meet a number of people who were at the heart of surfing in the UK, hence Gwynedd's journey to London in the company of other luminaries such as Linda Sharpe, Rodney Sumpter and Steve Daniel. Later, Gwynedd returned to competitive surfing one more time, entering and winning the English Surfing Championships in 1990.

"When I first started surfing, in the 1960s on the beaches of Newquay, I didn't have a wetsuit," says Gwynedd. "Some of the boys and men had long surf shorts; others cut old denim trousers to make shorts. In the autumn, we would wear woolly jumpers. Wetsuits changed everything. I can remember when someone started making them and selling them on Towan beach from a van. But if it's a hot and sunny day, it's a lovely feeling to surf without a wetsuit."

It's not hot and it's not sunny at the World Bellyboarding Championships, but Gwynedd won't be wearing a wetsuit. Neither will any of the other competitors (the eldest of whom is an 89-year-old woman, while the youngest is a four-year-old boy), for here, wetsuits are strictly forbidden. But Newquay-based surf instructor Laura Hamblin, 25, has no doubt that whatever the weather, everyone is set for a fun-packed day. "Bellyboarding is so much fun," she says. "When I first started riding a bellyboard, local surfers thought I was mad. But then a lot of them got into it. On days when the surf isn't so good you can still go out and have a blast, and on a bellyboard, every wave is overhead. You'll have way more tube rides than on a conventional surfboard."

Sally Parkin, the founder of the Original Surfboard Company, emerges from the expression session. Blue eyes intense and ablaze, salt water dripping from an all-in-one 1920s, woollen navy bathing suit, she speaks fervently to John Isaac, a well-known British surfing photographer. "It's not bellyboarding. It's surf riding. That's what it used to be called, and that's what it should still be called. And it's just as much fun as stand up surfing."

Advertising executive Matt McGregor-Mento, who has travelled from New York for the event, adds his view. "Bellyboarding chimes with a rethinking of surf culture generally. We've reached a point in our surfing evolution where we recognise that we're not all pros, busting the lip and getting shacked. We're reassessing how to have fun in the water, what to ride, where and when." Matt avows that "Pound for pound, you can have more fun on a bellyboard than any other kind of surfcraft."

Gwynedd smiles. She has seen it all before. "I remember Phoebe Lean from Saltash. She used to take the train to Newquay to enjoy the waves of Tolcarne with her wooden bellyboard. I knew her when she was well into her 80s, still going to the sea. She designed her own board by cutting it in half and drilling holes in it, so that it could be tied together with string. She did this so that when she went to Australia to visit relatives she could pack her bellyboard in her suitcase."

In 2005, Gwynedd entered the World Bellyboarding Championships for the first time – and won the ladies' division. She tends to bellyboard instead of surf when it is high tide and busy at the Newquay breaks she has surfed for 50 years, but would rather stand-up surf. "It's lovely to see people enjoying the sea, whatever they're doing and whatever craft they're using. But for me, stand-up surfing is still the best."

For Gwynedd, there are many reasons to keep surfing. "There are lovely moments in the sea as you're waiting for waves: listening to the birds and watching them in flight and seeing them dive for fish; seeing fish skim along the top of the water in the gleaming sun; first thing in the morning, seeing the moon still there and the sun breaking through the red sky; seeing the odd seal popping his head up as if to say hello; seeing dolphins. At sunset, there's a kind of peace as the sun sets and the waves continue to push gently through. I also like the black mood of the clouds when it's raining; the way they're replaced by the sun and then small rainbows can be seen through the waves."

It's time for Gwynedd's heat. She walks confidently to the sea, board under her arm. It's a walk she has taken all her life, one that she will take time and again for as long as she can, one that has seen her meet and know surfers of all kinds, from Laird Hamilton to Russell Winter, from her closest surfing friend Ernest Martinez to a who's who of Newquay stalwarts over the years; from pioneers like Jack Lydgate and Bob Head to Graham Nile, Nigel Semmens, Minnow Green and Chris Jones, onto Alan Stokes and Grishka Roberts, whose father, Trevor, said he would only teach Gwynedd if she managed to carry a heavy 10 ft Malibu board to the water's edge on her own.

"Trevor was a big man and surfed very well, as did Jack Lydgate, who was originally from Hawaii. They were both lifeguards on Tolcarne beach. I remember being a young girl, watching in amazement as they stood up and rode waves. I was determined to have a go, and my brother had managed to borrow a board. So I put it on my head and walked to the sea and off I went with Trevor."

After Gwynedd's heat, the black clouds give way to sunshine for the remainder of the World Bellyboarding Championships.

BAD BOY BOBBY AND THE NEW YORK QUIKSILVER PRO

Bobby Martinez looks like a boxer. Bobby Martinez is a boxer. And when elite pro surfing came to New York, Bobby Martinez didn't pull his punches.

Some surfers are media friendly. They turn up on time for interviews, behave courteously and sometimes even seem to like the journalists who write about them. Other surfers are not so media friendly. They fail to show up for interviews, or if they deign to favour a humble scribe with their presence, proceed to mumble inarticulately and seem wholly uninterested in their interlocutor's questions. This latter breed is dying as surfing's metamorphosis to mainstream cash

Plate 1 Mark Visser surfing Jaws, Maui, at night, 2011. (Photograph taken by Erik Aeder)

Plate 2 78ft and a world record: Garrett McNamara at Nazaré, Portugal (© Wilson Ribeiro/NazaréQualifica)

Plate 3 Nigel Veitch (right) at Watergate Bay, Cornwall, with future World Champion Martin Potter, during the Euro-Pro Contest, 6 August 1985. (© Neil Watson)

Plate 4 Carlos Burle paddling heavy Gurlen Rock, Bundoran Bay, October 2006 (© Al Mackinnon/www.almackinnon.com)

Plate 5 Big wave charger Tony Butt among the big stuff in northern Spain (© Jakue Andikoetxea/3sesenta)

Plate 6 Being Dave Rastovich makes for ultra stylish cutbacks like this (© Simon Buck/www.simonbuckphotography.com)

Plate 7 Russell Winter: arguably Britain's greatest ever surfer (© Mike Newman/Ocean-Image.com)

Plate 8 Buttons Kahuliokalani with the author – and The Last Tree on Earth (© Alex Wade)

Plate 9 Greg Long charging hard at Dungeons, South Africa, one of the world's heaviest waves (© Al Mackinnon/www.almackinnon.com)

Plate 10 Craig Holly and Kye Fitzgerald at East Strathy, Scotland after 1,300 miles in a very small car (© Alex Williams)

Plate 11 Agatha Christie, Waikiki 1922 (© The Christie Archive/Museum of British Surfing)

Plate 12 Miki 'Da Cat' Dora at J-Bay, South Africa: still stylish in the autumn of his surfing years (© Mike Newman/Ocean-Image.com)

Plate 13 Rik 'Peg Leg' Bennett: not stopping surfing any time soon (© Greg Martin)

Plate 14 Kelly Slater pulling in to solid La Graviere, France, September 2005 (© Al Mackinnon/www.almackinnon.com)

Plate 15 Riding waves with dolphins will have you stoked for days (© Mike Newman/Ocean-Image.com)

Plate 16 The beauty of bodysurfing is distilled perfectly in Keith Malloy's film *Come Hell or High Water* (© Chris Burkard and Come Hell or High Water)

cow gains momentum in the early 21st century, but still, not every elite surfer is on message.

And then there's Bobby Martinez.

When the Association of Surfing Professionals (ASP) rolled into New York in September 2011 for the city's inaugural Quiksilver Pro, the surfing world was in two minds. There were those who thought the event was a great idea because it would bring surfing to a much bigger audience. A rise in profile would be good for the ASP's bank balance and have a commensurately bulging effect on its competitors' wallets. The big surf wear brands – who in effect, run the World Tour as its financial backers – also stood to gain, as swathes of suitably inspired Big Apple residents would take to Manhattan's high streets in search of surfing apparel. As Quiksilver CEO Bob McKnight put it, surfing was coming to "the largest media arena in the world". What was not to like?

On the other hand, there were those who said that the New York event showed that surfing was losing, or had actually lost, its soul. They claimed that the ASP's decision to host an event on the World Tour at Long Beach was meretricious. Sure, Long Beach gets waves, but if they're ever world class it's only in the depths of winter. This camp claimed that the best surfers on the planet should be brandishing their skills in the world's best waves, not places like Long Beach or another venue for the 2011 Tour – Ocean Beach, San Francisco, a beach-break next to a teeming mass of people, but not a genuinely world-class wave.

And then there's Bobby Martinez.

From the beginning, Martinez was an anomaly. He grew up in a working-class area of Santa Barbara, California but despite learning to surf on waves that, as he says, "are pretty frustrating – they never get above head high" became so good that by the age of 12 he had won his first amateur championship. It was the first of seven wins; sure enough, Martinez then joined the World Qualifying Series (WQS) and just as inevitably, soon made it onto the World Championship Tour (WCT). His first year on the WCT in 2006, was the stuff of dreams: he won the Billabong Pro Tahiti, beating Fred Patacchia in the final, but later and more remarkably, dispatched Kelly Slater to win the Billabong Pro at Mundaka. Overall, Martinez – a Latino competing most of the time against Caucasian Australian and American surfers – did well enough to finish fifth, an incredible achievement for his debut on the WCT. No wonder he was the 2006 Rookie of the Year.

In other ways, even as he continued to blow minds with his stylish and yet powerful goofy-foot surfing, Martinez was different. He eschewed the après-surf party scene. He was married. He loved dogs. He was covered in tattoos and if Santa Barbara isn't exactly a ghetto, it has its gangs – and Martinez knew people in them. Members of his family had even been knifed. Maybe it comes as no surprise that Martinez also boxed. "I love boxing, have done since I was a kid," he says. "It's my favourite thing. I love it with a passion. I pretty much love it more than surfing."

But if, on flat days, he would keep fit physically and mentally by boxing, Martinez also brought a pugilist's attitude to his dealings with sponsors, ASP officials and even fellow surfers. Time and again he would fall out with them; not even a surfer of Slater's stature was safe from his barbs. Asked once if he thought the multiple world-champion was in danger of tarnishing his legacy by staying on the competition scene for too long, Martinez replied "I don't know and I don't care." For good measure, and alluding to Slater's ritual tease about whether he will complete a full year's WCT or not, he added: "I just hate how he says he's not doing the tour and then he does the whole year. Obviously he loves the spotlight, but to me I don't care what he does."

There was more. When the ASP was threatened by the prospect of a breakaway tour, Martinez unflinchingly spoke his mind. Stating that for him, the tour was about "surfing against the best, to maybe one day see your dream come true by winning amongst the best", he went on to embody a paradox: "I know the surfers as a whole. All it comes down to is money. No one cares what tour they're on, just as long as they can make the most money possible before they retire." He concluded his answer to ESPN Action Sports interviewer Jon Coen, who had asked him if he would support a breakaway tour, by saying: "If anyone wants the best surfers in the world to compete on one tour, all they have to do is put a lot more money for prize winnings and [the surfers] will all jump on board. That's the truth. I'll go with them too if I get an invite."

But in late 2009, the ASP did its best to forestall those who would create what was deemed the 'Rebel Tour'. Instead of the WCT and WQS, all surfers would fall under a 'One World Ranking', with the top 32, plus two wild cards, qualifying for the contests that decide the champion. Anyone who fell outside the top 34 would be cut mid-season, rather than at the end of the year-long season, as had been the effect of the division between the WCT and WQS. The idea – borrowed from professional tennis – was also intended to make surfing more exciting, but it didn't do anything for Martinez. He candidly admitted that he was baffled by the complex new ranking system (as was just about everyone outside the ASP), and said it was "the dumbest thing surfing has ever done".

As if this wasn't enough, in the same interview Martinez uttered the truth that dare not speak its name: surfing, as a spectator sport, is often incomprehensible and boring. "I think of it like this," Martinez told Coen. "Unless you surf, you're not going to [care] about surfing. No one cares how many off the lips you do to win a contest. The only people who care are the surfing fans and the die-hard surfers. Other than that, people don't care . . . it's just the fact. I've watched surfing with people from where I grew up, people who don't surf at all. They ask me, 'Why does everyone do the same thing?' That's just what it looks like when people don't know about surfing and don't care to know about it. They think this one-tier system will make more people watch surfing, but it's not going to do anything except confuse people about how the rating system works."

And then the Quiksilver Pro came to New York, with surfing's first $1 million prize purse. The crowds came, the cameras rolled, the waves did their best and everyone was happy. Until that is, Martinez – having knocked-out Australia's Bede Durbidge to set up a third-round heat against Slater – gave another interview. Only this time, it was beamed live to millions.

"The ASP and you guys aren't going to want this interview," said Martinez to Quiksilver marketing man Todd Kline. They certainly didn't. As Kline stood by, unable to summon the will to interject and alternately looking mortified and grinning helplessly, Martinez tore into the notion of New York hosting an elite surf contest. The following transcript of the interview, in which Martinez sounds and looks like a welterweight, trash-talking his opponent before a fight, is courtesy of Zach Weisberg's 8 September 2011 piece at www.theinertia.com:

> *"First of all, I'd like to say (an' the ASP are going to fine me) 'cuz I don't want to be a part of this dumb f*** ing-wannabe tennis tour. All these pro surfers want to be tennis players. They want to do a halfway cutoff. How the f** k is somebody who's not even competing against our caliber of surfers ahead of 100 of us on the one world ratings?*
>
> *"They've never been here. They've never f** king made the right to surf against us, but now we're ranked upon them. Come on now. Bullshit. That's why I ain't going to these stupid contests no more. This is my last one, because FTW, my sponsor, is here and I just tell it like it is. This is my last one, and I don't like tennis. I don't like the tour . . . Who gives a f** k? You know what I mean?*
>
> *"I've been here before. I love this city. I'll tell you right now, if my sponsor wasn't here, I wouldn't be here for this dumb contest. ASP? They f*** ing . . . surfing's going down the drain thanks to these people."*

The analogy Martinez made to professional tennis was apt: given the ASP's adoption of the rolling one world ranking system, the world's top 34 surfers could be outranked by competitors who had never surfed against them. But his rant did not go down well with the powers that be. Martinez was promptly suspended from the World Tour for breach of Article 151 of the ASP International Rule Book, which states that surfers shall not 'at any time damage the image of the sport of Surfing'. Interestingly, in notifying Martinez of its decision the ASP wrote "You are suspended from the ASP World Tour IMMEDIATELY."

Perhaps, in dealing with Martinez, ASP officials felt that capital letters were the *sine qua non* of punishment, but history has – partially, at least – vindicated the man from Santa Barbara. Later in 2011, the ASP's ranking system bewildered even its own statisticians when Slater was crowned champion at the Ocean Beach event. The Floridian would go on to clinch his 11th world title, but at that point had not done so. Cue ASP CEO Brodie Carr doing the decent thing and falling on his sword. Later that year, the ASP declared that it was dropping the midseason cut-off – that which had so enraged Martinez – and later still came more intriguing news: the New York event would go into hibernation for 2012, perhaps returning in 2013.

A backlash has since been evident. Many eminent surfing writers have criticised the ASP's handling of a number of things, ranging from its rankings system and the disparity between the spoils for male and female professional surfers, to the all-too-palpable desire to follow the money. And those same commentators have quietly noted that Martinez made a point that very few of his peers would have had the courage to make.

As for Martinez, he remains a conundrum. His tirade was delivered as he wore his sponsor's baseball hat. His sponsor's name? FTW, or, 'F*** the World'. FTW would have gained oodles of exposure thanks to its star rider's rant, but whether this was intended all along remains a matter of conjecture. What is not in doubt, however, is that Martinez surfs as a goofy-footer (with his right foot forward) and yet boxes in orthodox stance, with his left-foot forward. An orthodox boxer would surf as a natural footer, 99 per cent of the time.

But then again, there's nothing orthodox about Bobby Martinez.

THE BIG M

Legend, n. A person having a special place in public esteem because of striking qualities or deeds, real or fictitious.

We all remember our first surfboard. Not the first serious surfboard we owned but the one that first gave us the feeling of riding a wave. Even if we didn't know who made it or where it came from, we can recall how many fins it had, what colour it was, how long it was, whether it was full of dings and if it had a leash.

For some people, that first board will be the humble Swellboard, while for others it'll be the old Kamikaze shortboard that Dad is too old to ride anymore. It might be Mum's fat-railed minimal, or a K-Bay longboard which an older brother pushes into a wave. But in St Ives, in west Cornwall, the chances are that it'll be none of these. One board has towered over all others for 25 years, providing generations of the town's surfers with pleasure and, in equal part, pain. That board is not a board to mess with. It's a board that pulses with life and history. It is a legend.

That board is The Big M.

"The Big M has a life of its own," confirms Stef Harkon, who arrived in the town when The Big M was a mere twinkle in its shaper's eye. The Liverpool-born surfer and skater has been a fixture in the line-ups of West Penwith, but especially Porthmeor, for over a quarter of a century. He admits that when it comes to The Big M, "there is so much myth and legend surrounding it that it's difficult to know where truth and reality lie."

Where, then, to begin? There's nothing for it but to take a trip to St Ives to meet The Big M's current custodian – rugby player, fireman and surf school instructor John Navin. He promises he'll have The Big M ready for inspection, and doesn't disappoint. It's there at the Porthmeor Surf School where Navin, a rugby player with Redruth for 10 years and now St Ives, runs surfing classes throughout the summer. Not, mind you, that he takes anyone out on The Big M.

"The Big M is in semi-retirement at the moment," says Navin, "but in its current state it is a dangerous beast. It's more likely to inflict damage than joy, unless, that is, you're an experienced Big M rider."

Even a cursory glance at The Big M bears out Navin's fears. Its vital statistics are not too threatening – it's an 8 ft 8 inch x 22.5 inch Vitamin Sea board, bearing the initials 'CJ' – but its mouldering yellow deck and underside are scarred with more dings than a World War II tank. Some have been fixed – in the loosest sense of the word – with gaffer tape, but where once were fluid curves and rails, now there is little but an uneven, gnarled surface. To lie on The Big M would be like clasping the trunk of the most weathered oak tree in England, while to stand on it would be to feel one, if not both, of your feet sink into a crevice.

But The Big M has served St Ives' surfers well. "Generations of us have ridden The Big M," says Harkon. "The board lived down at the lifeguard hut and pretty much everyone has had their first waves on it." Harkon cites contemporary charger Tom Lowe as a Big M rider, along with Rip Curl ripper Jayce Robinson. "It's more difficult to think of who *hasn't* ridden The Big M," says Harkon. He reckons that from former St Ives surfer, now part-New Zealand, part-Sennen Cove based Charles Williams, to a young super-grom like Harry de Roth, via another big wave charger in the form of Gwenver lifeguard Matt Smith (not to mention the likes of Tim Whitfield, Tim Simons and Dane Hall), just about every St Ives surfer worth his name has ridden The Big M.

The board takes its name from a big letter M on its underside, but why, and where did it come from? Former St Ives surfer Darren Moran has the answers. "The board was bought about 25 years ago by Martin Haag, a rugby player who went on to play for Bath and England," says Moran. "He wanted to get into surfing but at about 6 ft 8 inches he was so huge that we needed to find a big board for him. One day we went to Newquay and saw this yellow Vitamin Sea board in North Shore. It had a big M on it which was perfectly suited to big Martin. He paid about £60 for it."

Moran says that The Big M went on surf trips all over Cornwall and doubled up, post surf, as a table for beers and food. As Haag's rugby career progressed he found that he was frequently away from St Ives, and so asked Moran to look after the board. Then Moran himself went off on a Sri Lanka surf trip and settled in Jersey, and so someone else had to look after The Big M. John Navin was that man, and his daughter Brooke is also among those to have caught waves on the board, but The Big M's principal place of residence has always been the Porthmeor lifeguard hut.

Harkon and Navin both say that, over the years, The Big M has caused its fair share of havoc. "It's rock hard and weighs a ton," says Navin. "It's careered into people and been responsible for a few mamings." Harkon himself has been on the receiving end of The Big M dispensing pain rather than pleasure. "I had to have a stitch in the top of my head thanks to The Big M," he says.

Navin says that The Big M will take to the waves again soon, though he can't help but recall the words of Airborne Surf Division's Paul Boufler, the last man to fix The Big M. "He said 'Don't bring it back again'," says Navin.

The chances are that The Big M will live to see another Porthmeor session, and that Boufler may once again have to try and give it another lease of life. But meanwhile, one question remains. Exactly who now owns The Big M?

For Darren Moran, it's simple. "Porthmeor owns The Big M," he says.

LORD THURSO, COOL IN CAITHNESS

Think politicians have no sympathy with surfers? Scotland's MP for Caithness, Sutherland and Easter Ross will make you think again.

Very few politicians know anything about surfing, but Lord Thurso, Member of Parliament for Caithness, Sutherland and Easter Ross, bucks the trend.

"I'm not a surfer myself but I watch them with a telescope through my window," says the Eton College and Oxford University educated hereditary peer, whose house and land overlook the reef at Thurso East, a right hand reef break which is a contender for Britain's best wave. "Twenty years ago there were hardly any surfers here, 10 years ago a few more started turning up, and now there are always a few black dots out in the water. Their standard goes up dramatically every year."

In accordance with Scottish law on hereditary titles, Lord Thurso owns not only an estate which has been in his family since the 1680s, but also the rocks in front of Thurso castle, right down to the low water mark. "In England, the convention is different," he says. "English titles provide for ownership to the high water mark." However, fortunately for local and visiting surfers, not to mention the organizers of the O'Neill Highland Open, his lordship is not bothered by people using his land to go surfing. The Highland Open was first held at Thurso East in 2006, but Lord Thurso never once asked O'Neill for payment in return for the use of the land and the rocks during the contest.

"My family has a long-standing tradition of not interfering with people's enjoyment. I'm just pleased to see that there is so much fun going on in the water outside my window."

John Thurso comes from a venerable Liberal Democrat family. His grandfather, Sir Archibald Sinclair, was the Liberal Party leader from 1935 to 1945, and it was following his father's death in 1995 that John took his seat in the House of Lords. He has since spoken many times in the House of Lords in favour of Lords reform, and made a piece of constitutional history in 2001 when he became the first hereditary peer to be elected to the Commons having previously sat in the Lords.

After studying, Lord Thurso went on to have a distinguished career in the hospitality industry. Since 2001, he has been a full-time politician. The last O'Neill Highland Open to be held in Thurso took place in 2011, and its disappearance from the remote, wind-and-rain lashed Scottish town is likely to have dismayed Lord Thurso. He is on record as having said that the Highland Open was "a brilliant thing to have on the town's doorstep. It brings very good spend into the town, and from talking to people and hoteliers, I know that they're very appreciative of the event. It makes for something new and different, encouraging a fresh perspective on Scotland so that tourism isn't just about traditional pursuits such as hill-walking and fishing. Moreover, everyone here loves meeting the surfers. It's a cliché but it's true – they're a really nice bunch of people."

Moreover, "surfing is a great thing for young people to get into," says Lord Thurso.

But despite his enthusiasm, despite the annual influx of Hawaiian, Australian, South African and Brazilian surfers, despite the hordes of British surfers who make pilgrimages to Thurso on a regular basis, and for all the increasingly high profile of surfing in Scotland, Lord Thurso is not tempted to join the black dots in the water.

"I was brought up swimming in the sea outside the family home in just a pair of trunks, but I fear the experience may have scarred me for life. Mind you, if I'd had the kind of kit O'Neill makes today, I think I'd have given it a go."

It may be too late for Lord Thurso to take up surfing, but his willingness to assist in holding the Highland Open, allied with his acceptance of surfers coming and going on his land, marks him out as that rare, and rather cool, breed: the politician who understands surfing.

A DEBT AT DUNGEONS

A trip to South Africa's premier big wave spot proves that camaraderie among big wave surfers also extends to the competitive world of surf photography.

Some big wave breaks have names that do them justice, while others are christened somewhere between the dull and the benign. Jaws, for example, neatly encapsulates the terror of surfing Maui's infamous reef. A similar sense of anxiety is inherent in the title of Mexico's offshore island wave, Killers, which is at the most northern of the two Islas de Todos Santos. Western Australia's Cyclops, seven hours from Perth and only accessible by boat, has a name to match the menace of its mutant lips. But there is no hint of danger in Cortes Bank, the shallow chain of underwater mountains in the Pacific which has seen a number of massive rides, especially by Californian Surfing Hall of Fame inductee Mike Parsons. Elsewhere, Maverick's – reputedly named after a German Shepherd puppy who tried to follow his owner into the line-up – sounds almost friendly, likewise Cloudbreak, one of Fiji's bigger contenders.

But in South Africa there is a break whose name puts it squarely in the spine-tingling category – before it's even been glimpsed. Step forward, Dungeons, so called by a local surfer who was ensnared underwater for a two-wave hold down. The waves which caught him were in the region of 25 ft, which makes for an awful lot of water from which to escape. Add the fact that, as famed big wave surfer Greg Long puts it, "the ocean is alive at Dungeons", and this is perhaps the most appositely named big wave spot of them all. Moreover, get it wrong at Dungeons, and if the monstrous amount of white water doesn't kill you, a great white shark might: here, they're as common as seals.

Sitting outside Hout Bay, Cape Town, in the shadow of the towering Sentinel Mountain, Dungeons comes alive between May and October, thanks to storms generated by the Roaring Forties. Its right-handers start to work at 10 ft, but Dungeons can hold waves of over 40 ft. The wave was first surfed in 1984 by two Cape Town surfers, Pierre de Villiers and Peter Button, but it wasn't until the 1990s that it began to be surfed regularly. Then, and into the first decade of the 21st century, a crew which includes Ian Armstrong, Cass Collier, Mickey Duffus and Chris Bertish, put Dungeons on the map. Bertish at one stage almost lost his life in the process – he was knocked unconscious by his board while trying to paddle through a set wave. Bertish had been underwater for 45 seconds, and only quick work by fellow surfers Ross Lindsay and Pierre Du Plessis saved him.

Surf photographer Al Mackinnon had heard all about Dungeons. "I'd read about it, and seen video footage," he says. "It looked horrible, unpredictable and lumpy – just downright ugly." When he finally got there, his apprehension was confirmed. "It's a very spooky place, capricious and shifty. I didn't like the look of it at all."

Mackinnon was lured to Dungeons in July 2006. The draw was the Red Bull Big Wave Africa contest which was held annually at Dungeons between 24 July and 31 August for 10 years from 1999, until Red Bull decided to put the event into what it termed 'hibernation'. This decision was deplored by many South African big wave surfers, not least the up-and-coming and notoriously fearless Frank Solomon. "Red Bull did it for 10 years and they kind of decided that's it. It's terrible," he told Cyrus

Saatsaz, writing for *The Inertia.* "[The contest] was a platform for the young South African guys to do well. Now we have to go somewhere new where people don't really know us and start from scratch. It sucks, but you know I really want to [surf big waves] so whatever, I'm going to keep doing it."

Solomon's dismay is all the more understandable because it unwittingly brings into focus another facet of big wave surfing: money. Big waves can mean big cash – Mike Parsons pocketed $66,000 for his 2001 ride of a 66 ft wave at Cortes Bank – but the surfers doing the charging aren't the only ones who stand to profit. For the legions of photographers who converge at places like Dungeons for international events, capturing the best ride, the deepest barrel and the biggest wave can be career-changing. Strangely though, it was only after the dust had settled on the Red Bull Big Wave Africa event that Mackinnon found himself in pole position. And more to the point, what ended up being a photograph of Greg Long's ride in the following year's Billabong XXL Biggest Wave category, was down to a rare act of generosity in what is often a cut-throat world.

"I arrived at Kommetje, a district of Cape Town, the night before the Red Bull competition was set to run," explains Mackinnon. "I awoke after just a few hours' sleep but as soon as I got to the event site, which was still in darkness, there was a real buzz. A lot of the world's top big wave riders were milling around, and more were set to arrive during the morning. A surf check was done and the decision was made: it was a green light, the Red Bull Big Wave Africa was on.

"At this point I was a little confused as it appeared from the charts I'd seen that the swell would build during the day and the conditions looked set to be far better the next morning, with light offshore winds and 20 ft surf. The scenery was breathtaking, the sets were about 12-15 ft, the sun was shining and with light winds it seemed almost pleasant at Dungeons. But you could see what a volatile wave it could be. It seemed to be all over the place, with huge shifting peaks firing as if the reef acted like a shotgun.

"Sure enough the swell steadily increased in size and the final was held just in time before the wind came up from the south-east and hacked the line-up to pieces. The hard-charging John Wittle from Durban put on quite a show and ended up taking home the cake. The other finalists were Chris Bertish and Andrew Marr. They were all South Africans, which was quite remarkable given the strong international field."

Mackinnon's hunch that the best was yet to come proved accurate. "I kept looking at the charts and was convinced that the days after the final would produce massive surf," he says. "Sure enough, Sunday brought the swell I'd been hoping for."

In fact, the day immediately after the contest proved to be better than the Friday when Wittle took first place. But Mackinnon resigned himself to watching from land. He couldn't find a boat to take him out to the line-up. Saturday night saw the local bars full of big wave surfers intent on capping their awesome session – Dungeons on Saturday had broken at 20 ft, in beautiful, clear sunshine – in style.

As is his wont – he is a tee-totaller, known for eschewing the party scene at surfing events and rising early – come Sunday morning, Mackinnon was up early. He was with Duncan Scott, another South African surfer known for his big wave surfing and, by way of a curious counterpoint, his devotion to surfing the Severn Bore. They found Kommetje "blanketed by sullen rain clouds, grey was everywhere, ocean, sky and land simply varying shades; it was a monochrome picture with the contrast set at minimum. After driving around it became apparent that everyone had been out drinking the night before, celebrating the previous day's feats. Pretty much everyone seemed to be still in bed. But as time wore on, the word began to filter out that the crews had been caught unawares: Dungeons was on again. Tow teams were converging from various corners of the Cape to Hout Bay and a glance at the line-up showed that they were right to be getting their acts together."

But Mackinnon seemed set for yet more frustration. It is possible to swim out to the line-up at Dungeons but it is also highly inadvisable given not just the distance, but the fact that the water is shark-infested. Surf photographers therefore hitch lifts on boats from Hout Bay harbour. But Mackinnon couldn't find a lift. "We were getting stone-walled. Nobody wanted to take us out on their boats. A South African photographer friend of Duncan's had got a commission from a big US title and had got a boat, but he wanted exclusivity. It meant he didn't want to know. I was effectively barred from the line-up. I thought that was that."

But it wasn't. By a stroke of good fortune Mackinnon ran into Shaun Timoney, a surf photographer from Kommetje. "Shaun was on his way out to Hout Bay," says Mackinnon. "He's a Christian. Maybe this had a bearing, I'm not completely sure. Whatever the exact reason, Shaun agreed to take us out in his little RIB."

Even so, Mackinnon recalls that Timoney "seemed to be in two minds. He was a freelance too. Because he didn't have a commission, he and I could end up sending our images to the same titles. The one way to make sure this didn't happen would have been to refuse to take me, but Shaun rose above whatever doubts he might have had. The weather was miserable, not quite the light conditions that photographers live for, but there was no time to lose, so I threw on my wetsuit, grabbed a camera and put it in a bin liner, chucked a fleece on and jumped into the tiny inflatable. Our crew consisted of Shaun and a friend of his called Nico, both locals, and myself and Duncan."

Things grew even more intense thanks to Nico.

"Nico was on driving duty and he liked driving – fast. He was clearly a bit of an adrenalin junkie. As we headed out into the South Atlantic in the steady rain and rounded the forbidding cliffs of the Sentinel, Nico seemed to drive faster and faster. We were bouncing from peak to peak across a liquid mogul field, the crew remonstrating as each impact sent a shock through our spines. He would slow down for a while before getting carried away once again, but there was an upside: it wasn't long before we reached the scene. Several boats with spectators and photographers were idling wide of the line-up while a handful of tow teams buzzed over the outer reef at Tafelberg, some way beyond the Dungeons line-up. There wasn't much going on there, but the absence of jetskis in the Dungeons line-up was a green light to a few chargers including Gary Linden, Grant Washburn and our own Nico and Duncan, who went for a paddle. This proved to be a mistake as the swell was steadily growing in size. Grant and Nico each copped serious hammerings. The paddle session proved to be short-lived as the decision was made to leave it to the tow teams.

"Suddenly the line-up seemed to empty. We had a conflab in the dingy. Something told me the weather was going to clear up a bit and I didn't want to miss anything that was still out there. Fortunately the lads concurred, so as the other boats headed back to land, their photographers satisfied with the day's spoils and spectators fed up with the cold wind and rain, we waited. Some decent rides were going down, but with a gusting cross-shore wind blowing rain straight into the lens, pictures were proving hard to come by. I spent my time rubbing water off the lens only for it to be awash again in a matter of seconds; at one stage I thought my camera had been killed by the rain.

"But all at once, the wind switched to a light offshore, the rain stopped and the cloud thinned at a touch – and then it happened. Grant 'Twiggy' Baker slung Greg Long into a giant of a wave and immediately I knew it was the one. He went on the first wave of the set and put everything on the line. The wave was beautiful. Somehow it hit the reef differently to the previous waves; the curves were just right. Greg skimmed down the face drawn smooth by the suck, laid down a bottom turn, the wave throwing the biggest tube I've ever seen and then, in an image I'll never forget, discharging the spit in the most ferocious show of energy. There was no time to digest what had just happened. Simon Lowe was on the next wave of the set. It wasn't as monstrous as Greg's wave but it was impressive in its own right. Simon lost it on the bottom turn and took a near direct hit. Before anything could be done to salvage him the next wave steamrollered through, this time with Mike Schlebach in the pocket. He casually pulled up into the barrel, standing proud, but the lip was too quick and in the blink of an eye he was 30 yards back in the pit and getting deeper by the moment. We lost sight of him, still holding his line as the beast engulfed him.

"Simon and Mike were eventually fished from the depths, still in one piece. The next day, all involved met up at Shaun's house and went through a slideshow of the photos. It was only then that we realized we'd managed to record the most gigantic surf ever ridden on the African continent."

The resulting images catapulted Mackinnon into a bidding war involving the international surfing press. The two premier US titles, *Surfer* and *Surfing*, emerged as the front runners for the rights. *Surfer* came up with the best offer for the US rights, and worldwide total deals ultimately netted a sum comfortably into five figures. And then, in the Billabong XXL Awards for 2007, further kudos came when Long's Dungeons' ride won the Biggest Wave category. The same session also saw video footage shot by Grant Washburn enable Andrew Marr to take second place in the Ride of the Year category.

Long and Mackinnon have since gone on to work often together, and Mackinnon has established himself as one the most talented surfing photographers of his generation. But in the fiercely competitive world of surf photography, he knows that he will always be in debt to Shaun Timoney.

"I went out to California for the Billabong XXL Awards night and was reunited with Shaun and his lovely wife Lucinda at the ceremony in Orange County. It was an incredible night and I was delighted to split my prize money with Shaun: if he hadn't been the bigger man and allowed me to join him that day, it would never have happened."

AFTER *RIO BREAKS*

The filming of *Rio Breaks* at Arpoador beach in Rio de Janeiro looked set to transform the lives of two boys who lived in the notoriously dangerous 'Vietnam' part of the Cantagalo favela. But what happened next?

At www.urbandictionary.com, the definition of a favela is uncompromising: 'A Brazilian ghetto, the toughest neighbourhood you would ever want to find yourself in. Makes American ghettos and barrios look tame. Even the police are afraid to enter.'

Anyone who has seen *City of God*, the 2002 crime drama directed by Fernando Meirelles and Kátia Lund, would concur. The acclaimed film depicts the growth of organized crime in the Cidade de Deus suburb of Rio de Janeiro between the end of the 1960s and the beginning of the 1980s. Its portrayal of life in one of the city's many shantytowns is honest, unflinching and disturbing. Rio may be the city with the most imposing statue of Christ in the world, known as Christ the Redeemer, which is perched at the peak of the Corcovado mountain overlooking the city, but godliness in the favelas is hard to find.

Justin Mitchell and Vince Medeiros, director and co-writer/producer respectively, were drawn to a favela in Rio called Cantagalo for their 2009 film, *Rio Breaks*. Specifically, they were drawn to a slum area of Cantagalo nicknamed 'Vietnam'. Their film tells the story of two boys, Fabio, 13, and Naama, 12, who live in Vietnam (so christened because of the daily backdrop of shootouts between rival gangs), but who spend much of their time at nearby Arpoador beach. The expanse of the sea, visible from their homes on the hillside, is both a literal and metaphorical expression of freedom and escape for the boys, likewise their enjoyment of childlike pursuits like flying kites and playing marbles. But try as they might to evade its snare, the endemic violence of the favela is every bit as compelling as the ocean. Fabio's father has died because of gang violence, and his mother has abandoned the family. The constant, palpable fear is that something equally dire could be the destiny for Fabio – and, perhaps, Naama. At a critical juncture in their upbringing, the boys walk a tightrope between innocence and adulthood, between avoiding being sucked into a life of crime and embracing a fate that is as inexorable as it is undesirable.

But surfing arrives in the boys' lives, and the sea takes on yet another meaning. It becomes the source not merely of escape – of something glimpsed from their cramped abodes on the hillside – but of hope. If the brooding Fabio and easy-going Naama can see through their involvement with the Favela Surf Club on Arpoador beach and become surfers, there is something for them beyond Vietnam. If they can stay fit through surfing that will be an achievement; if they can regularly attain the sense of joy that surfing brings, even better; and if they can win contests and become sponsored, perhaps there is another life for them, one far, far away from the favela.

One scene perfectly encapsulates this. We see Fabio, a goofy-footer, racing down the line of a peeling left-hander on a bright and sunny day, then sitting on the beach as the sun sets, looking melancholy as he speaks in Portuguese to the camera, the subtitles revealing: "I don't really like living there. There are too many shootings and you are risking your life." And then, as Fabio is filmed paddling for a wave (with the camera behind him, looking towards the white sand of the beach), we see him go to pop up and then, as he is obscured by a surging mass of water, the words "I'd love to be able to leave" appear on the screen. The question is stark. Will Fabio make the drop – will he make the wave – or will the sun set on his dreams?

In *Rio Breaks,* surfing is about much more than 'having fun' (the pro surfers' vacuous stock interview answer to questions about the 'meaning' of surfing). It is about survival. Survive and surf the boys do, even meeting one of Brazil's most famous surfers, big wave charger Carlos Burle. But the film's ending is bittersweet. Naama, always the sunnier of the two, seems to be well on the right track. His smile is as open and ingenuous as ever, and his commitment to surfing is certain. But Fabio, the trickier of the two, seems to be drifting away from surfing. And in the favela, that can mean only one thing. Rather like Kate Chopin's narrator in *The Awakening*, he seems to be about to accept the embrace of something that will kill him.

After the release of *Rio Breaks* (which was justly lauded in many quarters), the boys' fates seemed to grow yet more divergent. In 2010, Luciano Huck, the host of one of Brazil's most popular TV shows, saw the film and liked its story. He decided to make a difference. His Saturday night show *Caldeirão do Huck* is an institution in Brazil, drawing millions of viewers each week, and Huck put young Naama on it. He is shown, at his tiny family house in the favela, talking about surfing and saying that he would love not only to surf in Hawaii but also to meet Kelly Slater, the greatest surfer of all time. Huck says he will take Naama to Hawaii and introduce him to Slater. In exchange though, Naama has to promise that he will not join the drug gang, keep going to school and agree to learn English.

Naama keeps his side of the bargain. When he meets Slater, his sincerity, so beguiling in *Rio Breaks,* is undiluted even though he is now in the midst of adolescence and has, in the years before the film, witnessed his brother's death at the hands of the police. He breaks down when he meets Slater, in a poignant and moving scene, but Huck's goodwill does not end in Hawaii. Back in Rio, Huck buys Naama's family a new house, away from the favela. Better yet, the TV presenter also goes on to refurbish the surf club. It becomes the cultural and sporting hub of life in the favela, while Naama becomes a local star.

But what of Fabio – so scarred, so tormented, so full of life and energy and so stoked, for a while at least, by riding waves? Vince Medeiros, himself from Brazil and the publisher of a magazine which, despite its name (*Huck*), bears no relation to his countryman, has good news:

"Fabio disappeared for a while, yes. The club didn't know what had become of him, or what he was up to, and I couldn't get any reliable information. But it seems that surfing is in his blood. I've heard that he's back on the beach, and that he's riding waves again, which is hugely encouraging."

And then, three years after the release of *Rio Breaks*, came another remarkable development. Global sports brand Nike signed a contract with the Favela Surf Club, agreeing to pay eight of its best surfers to teach some 50 favela children to surf, four hours a day, five days a week, all year round, for five years. Equipment, boards and wetsuits have been provided, and everyone at the club is the proud owner of Nike 'Favela Surf Club' lycra jerseys. The daily buzz on the beach is extraordinary, and there is hope, where previously there was none, for young people who are brought up in some of the most difficult circumstances imaginable.

It's all down to surfing. Just do it? Why not: it's worked a treat in Rio de Janeiro.

PART SIX

Worldwide Waves

SEVEN GHOSTS

The average surfer rides the average wave for 30 seconds. In Sumatra, on a river in the Kampar Peninsula, the average surfer can ride an average wave for 30 minutes – and counting. But is it true?

Teluk Meranti is in the Riau province of Sumatra, Indonesia. Around 2,500 people live in the small village, which lies on a bank of the Kampar River. Their average monthly income is around $200; historically, it came mostly from fishing. More recently, as the rainforest of the Kampar Peninsula has been decimated in search of its two main cash crops – acacia trees and palm oil – some villagers have made a living from logging. Others have taken to harvesting and exporting swallow's nest soup, a delicacy in Hong Kong and China. And thanks to a trip co-ordinated by Australian surfwear company Rip Curl – the brand behind 'The Search' – there are now some residents in Teluk Meranti who earn a crust thanks to surfing.

"It was the most radical, bizarre, intense and surreal surf trip of my life," says James Hendy, Rip Curl's marketing manager for South East Asia. "We were 70 km up-river, in the middle of nowhere, with no one anywhere near us for miles. There was nothing but jungle – or the remains of jungle – all around. And then, out of nowhere, comes this incredible wave. I've never experienced anything like it. I doubt I ever will again."

Hendy was in charge of organising what proved to be Rip Curl's most extraordinary search in years. It was one that came with more than a touch of responsibility, given the team of surfers he had assembled: Australian pro Dean Brady, a man whose motto is 'If you're not first, you're last'; Tyler Larronde from France, then just 16, but today, just over a year later, with a *Surfer* magazine cover to his name thanks to a ride at Jaws; Brazilian Bruno Santos, 2008's Billabong Tahiti Pro winner; and Oney Anwar, a young Indonesian ripper who has a major role with Rip Curl in Asia. As well as them, Hendy had to look after one of surfing's icons – three-times world champion Tom Curren, a man of few words (he once answered "Yeah" to every question put to him by a journalist), but seemingly infinite reserves of style and class.

"I didn't take it lightly," says Hendy. "There was a huge amount of planning for the trip but no matter how much we tried to cover off every eventuality, we couldn't. Things just kept happening. Things changed, things went wrong. There were plenty of times when I asked myself what I'd feel like if it became truly disastrous, if something happened to any of the guys. I didn't want to go down in history as the man who got Tom Curren killed."

In the end, it was Hendy who nearly lost his life in what was his first experience of surfing a tidal bore. "I'm from England, but had never surfed the Severn Bore, or any other bore," says Hendy, himself a talented surfer. Before he decamped to Bali, he was well-known as one of the best in the line-up at Porthleven, a Cornish reef break with decidedly clearer water than that which the Rip Curl team found on the River Kampar. "In Cornwall, at places like Porthleven or my old home break of St Agnes, you can see the bottom of the sea. You can't see further than an inch at the River Kampar. It's soupy, murky and mud-brown, all the way."

Before Hendy and his team arrived at Teluk Meranti they knew they wouldn't be surfing the translucently clear waves of surf film fantasy, but that was about the extent of their knowledge. "A French surfer called Antony Colas was the first to surf the waves on the River Kampar," explains Hendy, "but the locals have a name for the tidal bore that casts doubt in everyone's minds. They call it the 'Bono'. You can't help but have the name in mind when you're there; you can't help but wonder if you'll get a wave or if the whole thing's a myth."

Tom Curren elaborates. "Apparently the meaning of the word '*bono*' is 'it's true'. It comes in a conversation when somebody's describing the wave, and the other person says 'no, that's not true, it's impossible', then the other person says 'oh yeah, it is possible, it's true'."

Hence then, the 'Bono', a wave which for centuries Indonesians feared, as much as they wondered what caused it and where it came from. No wonder, in 2005, the Bono proved to be all too real when it swept away a speedboat and killed 14 people. Before and since, people have been taken unawares by a bore which originates in the shallow estuary of the river, thanks to a confluence of moon and tide, and then travels up to 130 km inland. The Kampar's shape acts as a natural funnel, and if, because of its deep water location, the wave is not visible at Teluk Meranti, downriver waves are generated which travel at speeds between 5 km per hour (in shallow sections) and 25 km per hour. Faces of up to 12 ft are possible, and it's believed that rides could last for up to four hours. Either side of the river, the wave sweeps away anything that is in its path, from trees and boats to people.

Antony 'Yep' Colas, a bore-riding aficionado, first surfed the River Kampar in 2010. Along with his brother Fabrice, Yep is renowned for surfing tidal bores around the world, from the Mascaret in France and the Severn in England, to Brazil's Pororoca and the River Qiantang in China. His experience made him a natural choice as event manager for the Rip Curl search of March 2011; a mission that entailed the use of three Zodiac boats, two jetskis, a helicopter and a substantial support crew.

The extensive equipment list and degree of logistical plotting may strike purists as taking the trip away from the quintessential surfer's search, one that sees the intrepid rewarded with immaculate, pristine waves thanks to a willingness to trek into the unknown. Helicopters and jetskis aren't usually part of the programme. In the archetypal search, the surfer is accompanied only by the rudiments of civilisation and a certain lack of materialism which helps propitiate the swell gods. However, when it came to Sumatra's Kampar Peninsula, serious equipment was needed for a serious search – without it, this particular surf trip would probably have been doomed. Hendy says, "Teluk Meranti is five hours from Pekanbaru, which is the capital of the Riau province and it's as remote as you can get. Dengue fever is a real problem and we needed to have a way to get to good medical attention if necessary. Add to that the fact that it took us an hour to get downriver to catch the wave. Without boats and jetskis we couldn't have done it. That's not even to mention the crocodiles."

Even the most hardcore surfer would agree that a jetski might come in handy when it comes to sharing a line-up with crocodiles. If the inhabitants of the Kampar Peninsula sometimes questioned the veracity of the tidal bore, they were under no illusions about what lurked in the murky river. "We were told that crocodiles weren't near Teluk Meranti itself, but that we'd find them the further away from the community we went," says Hendy. "Sure enough, on the second day, Tom and I were in one of the Zodiacs when we saw what looked like a huge log drifting in the water. The thing is, it had bubbles. The river was like glass and we got a perfect view of a crocodile that must have been at least four metres long." The vision lingered. "In the back of my mind every time a surfer came off, or if we capsized a boat, or whenever a jetski stalled, I remembered that croc," says Hendy.

And of thrills and spills – capsizes, wipeouts, losing control of jetskis – there were plenty. "On the first day the engine stalled in the boat as I was driving it," says Hendy, with a shake of his head. "We'd been waiting for the bore, sitting in the middle of the river, when suddenly we could hear the sound of hundreds of birds. They were taking off, getting out of the way as the wave came. Then we saw the wave. It was like a mirage at first."

Brady agrees. "We were sitting there and I was looking around, and it was just like any normal river. I couldn't really believe that the waves could happen. It's just not normal. But then it came."

Hendy again, "All we could see was a haze of white water that didn't seem to be moving. But, sure enough, it was moving. Soon we could see spray surging off the sides of the riverbank up into the air, and trees and bushes being flattened by what looked like the torrent of a waterfall, only one that was moving horizontally, straight for us. It struck me then just how strange the whole thing was. I mean, how many people deliberately sit in the path of a genuine tidal wave? Then the engine stalled and I had other things to think about; the first wave hit me and flipped the boat over. I got away with that incident – just."

The crew spent five days on the River Kampar, scoring 6-12 ft waves which peeled perfectly, on and on, seemingly forever. One image especially stunned all present, the sight, on day two, of seven flawless, 6-8 ft left-handers making up the head wave and driving towards the waiting surfers at over 25 kmh. "We coined the name 'Seven Ghosts' there and then," says Hendy. "It was just so surreal, like a hallucination, to see seven perfect waves coming towards us, unridden and inviting, and yet with the jungle all around."

But if this particular search yielded not only confirmation of the Bono, but also – caught on film – tube rides galore and even, courtesy of Oney Anwar, an aerial, it was anything but the average surf trip. Often the crew would hit sandbanks and be forced to wade in knee-deep water, pushing the boats for hours at a time, all the while hoping not to run into a crocodile; on one occasion they lost a jetski when its driver stalled on a wave and then got washed off (the jetski was recovered 10 km downriver). Anwar was not the only surfer to get barrelled but, as Bruno Santos put it, tubular bliss on the River Kampar was not conventional; rather, it was a case of "everything being black inside".

Hendy's patience, as the man in overall charge, was constantly tested. "It was pure chaos. Nothing went to plan whatsoever." Least of all the events on the last day, when the crew set off with two aims – to see Anwar airborne, and to enable Curren to set a world record for the longest ride. The first had just been achieved when the engine on the Zodiac being piloted by Hendy cut out. "I had Tom on board and a cameraman. There was nothing we could do. The wave hit us. Tom jumped out just before and ended up getting a four-mile ride, but things didn't go so well for me."

Hendy's boat was upside down. The powerful current pushed the Zodiac into an inlet, which only exacerbated Hendy's problems. "The bore flooded into the inlet, hitting its beach and then creating a refraction wave which came straight back at us. We had no control and were being tossed around helplessly, but by this stage it was almost funny."

Not so, what happened next. The two jetski drivers came over to help, and ropes were attached to one side of the boat, the idea being to pull it away and flip it back into its normal position. On the first attempt the boat spun round violently – and Hendy had an unplanned, and very dangerous, liaison with the propeller. "I could see it slashing down and thought it was going to take my head off. By a miracle it just glanced me, but it cut my ear in half. There was blood everywhere. It could so easily have staved my head in."

Hendy made it back to base camp at Teluk Meranti, where a doctor stitched up his ear. The rest of the crew survived, but only just: a similar incident with an upturned boat and a loose propeller almost killed one of the cameramen, too. By the end of the fifth day, everyone on this particular search was, as Anwar put it, "rattled" – and ready to go home.

"It was an amazing trip," says Hendy, "and the wave is real. It exists, and it's pretty near to perfect." But while now there is a dedicated surf camp (called Bono Surf) at Teluk Meranti, complete with a longboard, 7 ft shortboard and stand-up paddleboard and helping to provide extra employment for the locals, Hendy is in no rush to return. Summing up his experience of the Bono, the tidal bore that turned out to be all too true, Hendy says:

"I was just stoked to get out of there alive."

HOKKAIDO – THE RIGHTS OF PASSAGE

A respectful trip to Japan reveals that sometimes, as Haruki Murakami puts it in *Kafka on the Shore*, 'silence . . . is something you can actually hear'.

Chris Nelson, a former surf magazine editor turned writer, hails from Yorkshire. An upbringing surfing the freezing reefs of England's north-east coast led to a lifelong love of cold empty waves and their fringe communities, but a trip to Vancouver Island in 2005 set him on an odyssey he'll never forget.

On Vancouver Island, Nelson met Wayne Vliet, whose tales of growing up as surfer in 1960s Canada, with home-made wooden boards, leaky dive suits and sneakers, were the stuff of the pioneering frontiersman. Nelson empathised with the pains the small number of local surfers went through for a few good waves, and an epiphany came, too: it struck him that many of Vliet's experiences would be shared with other surfing pioneers across the globe. The hook was set and the tall, lean and wiry Nelson set out on a three-year journey to find these hardy souls and tell their stories. His travels took him to surfing's coldest fringes and hardiest outposts.

The resulting book, *Cold Water Souls: In Search of Surfing's Cold Water Pioneers* is a critically acclaimed anthropological study of the cold water communities that have grown up around the planet's coldest shores and the surfers who ride their waves. The book tells the story of how the seeds of surfing took root and flourished in places from Northern California to Vancouver Island, from Alaska to Nova Scotia, and the US Eastern Seaboard to Iceland, Scotland, North East England and beyond. But it was a trip to Hokkaido, Japan's second largest island, that proved an object lesson in how to handle one of surfing's thorniest problems: how to protect one's breaks from exposure and consequential overcrowding.

"It was after midnight when I walked out through the sliding doors of a deserted Chitose airport," says Nelson. "The 50 people on my flight had evaporated into the night. I was alone. Doubts began to creep into the back of my mind. I had no number to call, no phone that worked here and I could barely string a few words of Japanese together. It had taken six months just to get this far, and I was here on trust. It had all started with an email to a contact in Tokyo – just four lines of polite prose setting out my case. The reply came swiftly – he didn't have an 'in' on Hokkaido, but he would ask around. Two weeks later hope arrived in my inbox, my man in Tokyo knew someone who knew someone. No names were exchanged, but everyone wanted to know more, a detailed plan of exactly what I wanted and why I was coming. After another couple of rounds of the interview process I was given the name of Taro Tamai, my local contact and, I hoped, my man on the ground."

Hokkaido is Japan's most northerly prefecture, an island the size of Ireland. In the winter its northern fringes are ice-locked, the land buried under several feet of snow. It is a place where winter sports brought the Olympics, where water sports brought solitude. Nelson explains its allure: "Coming from the grey cold of Britain's North Sea, I'd always been drawn to those communities which existed on the edge, on surfing's fringes. When I looked at Hokkaido on the world map, sitting as it does on a latitude to the north of Vladivostok, I knew that

I needed to get to this remote place. But there was no easy route in, no friendly sponsored pro surfer to act as a conduit from the outside world."

If Hokkaido's very remoteness was the source of its appeal for Nelson, that same quality meant that he had to act as respectfully as possible.

"Without a well-worn path to follow, it's a case of tread carefully. Through e-mail channels I'd laid out my mission. I was chasing tales, not swells. My visit would not be the vanguard of an influx of surf tourists. But I knew I was walking a fine line."

Nelson's arrival at Chitose airport was not initially promising. "So here I was, jetlagged, waiting, hoping that nothing had been lost in translation. After 20 minutes I dragged my boardbag outside into the glacial night air and stood, transfixed by my icy breath. In the distance I could see a figure approaching. It had a casual gait that seemed familiar. This must be my man. He approached slowly, but as I turned to greet him, he continued by with a nod and disappeared into the terminal taking my hopes with him. But seconds later a van swept up to the curb. 'Chris? Hey, jump in,' beamed Yuki, who would be my driver on this quest to seek out the island's surfing pioneers.

"The next day I met Taro Tamai. Seated at his large, wooden kitchen table he poured hot water into the white porcelain teapot. Huge picture windows framed the volcanoes and peaks around us. As a Yorkshireman, I smiled at the shared symbolism of this simple act. Tea, the universal icebreaker." Taro is known as one of Japan's great snowboarders, an excellent free-rider who gracefully surfs the fields of champagne powder around his home. But what is less well known is that he is also a true soul surfer, often escaping the limelight in search of the isolated, freezing reefs and points on the island.

Nelson tuned in at once to what made Taro tick. "For Taro, being a cold water surfer is a holistic experience," he says. "It's not about wearing a thicker wetsuit and enduring – it's about where your mind takes you. The gradation in colour; the black and the white. It was this connection as cold water spirits, this shared understanding, that had gained me an audience."

But while there was a kinship between the two men, Nelson knew that he would not simply be ushered straight to Hokkaido's elusive reefs and points. He had to wait and was happy to do so.

"Sometimes it feels as though there is a demand for everything to be immediate. Travellers can pre-load, arriving drunk on facts. Go online before you go, check the swells, watch the videos, read the reviews. Check everything first. No need to communicate when you get there. There's a danger that we, as surfers, will become insular and removed from the very places and the very people we hope to experience. But take all this out of the equation, remove the digital drip and you have to engage, with the place, with the community. On Hokkaido, the language and the culture act as great filters. My journey so far had been a lesson in going slow, being patient. It reminded me of my days as a grommet in the north-east in the late eighties. You served your time and paid your dues on the beaches; then, when you had built up time and trust, you were invited to the secret reefs. It was a rite of passage, not an immediate right."

After three days of sharing stories and trading tales, Taro opened the door on his world.

"I had served my apprenticeship, and on my fourth day on the island, Taro offered to introduce me to Noboru, the very first waverider on Hokkaido."

Naminori is Japanese for surfing; Nelson was on course to meet its originator on Hokkaido.

"Under the stark, neon lights of a downtown Sapporo office, I was introduced to Noboru and another surfer called Kasagi. Without Taro we would not have been there. He'd had to reach out. He was personally vouching for me. But now we were a long way from the cosy surrounds of Taro's kitchen table. Nodding politely, we exchanged business cards, taking time to study them in turn, then placing them on the table. We sipped the strong, black espresso that is the lifeblood of Japan. Despite the formal surroundings there was a relaxed air – surfing has a way of bringing down barriers, be they linguistic or cultural. And soon the stories cascaded forth, Noboru part-narrating, part-translating.

"In 1976 he'd returned from the US, the stoke of surfing pumping through his veins. When he arrived home, there were no other surfers, no known surf breaks. No counter-cultural revolution. He had no pointers, no car. He was alone, but Kasagi was encouraged into the line-up. However they soon found themselves the centre of unwanted attention – the police started issuing threats, tickets and verbal warnings. In a land where strict rules and social pressures breed conformity, they didn't back down. Instead they recruited other potential, like-minded surfing souls. Japan's endemic motorcycle gangs offered access to a large pool of eager converts and strength in numbers."

"It was," says Nelson, "the cultural equivalent of Miki Dora recruiting Hells Angels to the Malibu line-up."

Kasagi showed him images across the table. Nelson says, "I saw Kodak prints in rich hues, reaching back through the decades to young surfers posing on the sand, leaning on the bonnets of surfboard-laden Datsuns and I was aware of my good fortune in being able to see these." He was privileged to have been given access to a rare and obscure realm, one from which he could have been barred at any time. Waves would surely follow on the trip, but better yet, Taro turned to explain that he and Nelson had been invited to eat at Kasagi's house. "Taro's whispered tone conveyed that this was an unexpected honour," says Nelson.

The surfers of Hokkaido had lifted the veil on their history and heritage, but they did so in a way that, for Nelson, was emblematic of how surfers should behave when it comes to the age-old issue of localism. "The Hokkaido surfers still shield their coastline's breaks from the fate suffered by many, but no one ever warned me off, as was the case in Nova Scotia; or told me not to write about their waves, as they had in Norway. There was no need. There was an implicit accord that we shared as cold water souls. Here, in a country where surfing still operates an honour system, access was a privilege. This was the right kind of localism in action. I knew from the off that if they'd wanted to shut me out, they could have done so at any time, and I would have been adrift. They could have just left me at the airport. Left me out in the cold."

1,300 MILES FOR A WAVE

Alex Williams is a veteran surf photographer who's used to plenty of travel. But one trip topped them all.

There are very few surf trips that Alex Williams has not done. Tall, solidly-built and now 56, Williams may hail from a sleepy village in south Devon but if a life could be measured in travel, his is as rich as they come. Williams has been to Hawaii at least 30 times, he's logged surf trips to just about every wave in Europe, has spent weeks at a time photographing surfers and windsurfers in the Caribbean and has racked up air miles to Indonesia, Australia, North and South America and Africa. Today, settled with his wife Sian, her son Asa and their baby daughter Tess, Williams is content to spend most of his time on the family farm at Bantham, his home from the age of six. But ask him which surf trip is his most memorable, and he grins wistfully.

"It was back in 1993," says Williams, "I had spent the summer covering surf contests in England and France and was in Hossegor, on the beach. It was about eight in the morning and I'd just watched

Derek Ho get a really nice barrel, when Derek Hynd wandered over. He waved a copy of a French newspaper at me and said it looked like there would be waves in Scotland. Derek was the marketing director of Rip Curl then, the man who pioneered 'The Search', media coverage which focused on discovering perfect waves in unusual locations. He was keen to see what Scotland had to offer and asked me what I thought of the chart. I looked at it and said 'Pretty good, but you'd better go and ask Carwyn Williams. See what he thinks'.

"Derek disappeared but came back a little later. He'd found Carwyn and said there was a big low coming in. He then asked me if I fancied a surf trip."

Williams chuckles. Perhaps the memory of Hynd, so free a spirit, so anti-corporate, so fiercely independent, taking advice from legendary Welsh surfer Carwyn Williams, strikes him as amusing. On the one hand because Hynd is not the sort to take advice from anyone, and on the other, because Carwyn's authoritative, source-of-all-wisdom side remains, to this day, kept largely under wraps. Be this as it may, the ensuing dialogue on the beach at Hossegor is cause for mirth:

"I asked Derek where he had in mind," says Williams. "He said 'Thurso'. I laughed out loud. How on earth would we get there, and who, if anyone, would be with us? Derek said: 'Be here at 2pm. We've got Craig Holly and Kai Fitzgerald.' They were both Rip Curl surfers, but no matter who they were or how good, the idea seemed crazy. There we were, in Hossegor in the late summer, and Derek reckoned we would somehow get to Thurso."

But Hynd is not the sort of man to make idle promises. He returned at 2 o'clock with a Renault 5 hire car.

"It was probably the smallest car I've ever been in for a surf trip," says Williams. But nevertheless, he, Kai (son of famous Australian surfer Terry, known as 'the Sultan of Speed'), Craig and Derek set off for Thurso. They drove through the night to Paris, and then to the northern French coast where they took a ferry to Portsmouth. Once in southern England, Hynd suggested a detour.

"We were heading north from the port when Derek said 'Isn't Stonehenge somewhere round here?' Of course, it wasn't that far away – not when you've already travelled over 600 miles – so off we went to see Stonehenge."

The pilgrimage complete, the journey continued. Again driving through the night, the quartet found themselves arriving in the Caithness town of Thurso at 5.30 the following morning. Dour, bedraggled and remote, Thurso is not a place on many tourists' maps. It is though, a cold water surfers' paradise, thanks to its exposure to the full force of Arctic swells that are driven irresistibly onto its flat, kelp-covered reefs. With Dounreay nuclear reactor nearby, and a neglected castle overlooking the reef-break of Thurso East, the surf break has an atmosphere all of its own, one only accentuated by the Orkney Island rock stack of the Old Man of Hoy, visible to the north, and undiminished by the name of its nearest wave – the 'Shit Pipe'.

Messrs Williams, Hynd, Fitzgerald and Holly had good reason to arrive in Thurso with hope of finding immaculate right-handers reeling across the reef. After all, the chart looked good and surely the surf gods would reward a journey of 1,300 miles?

Not so. "We drove up along the harbour and stopped at the seawall," recalls Williams. "What we saw was devastating. It was 1 ft, and onshore. There wasn't a surfable wave in sight."

But a surf trip with the man who invented 'The Search' was always unlikely to end in disappointment. Thurso's locals were duly asked where there might conceivably be waves. The answer was the east coast village of Skirza, some 25 miles away. Cramped in their Renault 5 and increasingly desperate, the four surfers headed east. There, in Sinclair's Bay, they found 4 ft, clean and perfect waves.

"We were over the moon," says Williams, again with a far-away smile. "Seals were in the water with us and the waves held up. We thought we were out of luck, but ended up scoring. It was fantastic."

Intriguingly, the Skirza surf trip was accompanied by a daily ritual too. "We stayed in a motel that had an old record player. The only LPs that were there featured Hawaiian songs. So every day, before we squeezed into the Renault 5 and drove to Skirza, Derek insisted on playing Hawaiian music. Looking back, it was surreal."

But was it worth it? "Yes," says Williams. "Travelling 1,300 miles for a wave was worth it. The trouble is, once the surf dropped off we had to drive all the way back." Still smiling, Bantham's most travelled, and surely most laid back surfer, adds an afterthought: "You know, I'm not sure I'd do it again."

ED'S LEFT, AKA THE SPOT WITH NO NAME

Nirvana is found on the coast of India – but what should it be called?

Ed Templeton was in a quandary. He'd just surfed on his backhand better than ever, he'd been all alone in the water, and he'd had an audience. They'd loved his every wave, cheering and clapping from the shore. Damn it, after a while some of them even got the hang of what he was doing so well that they climbed the rocky headland and whistled to let him know when the bigger sets were on their way.

Better yet, it was a sunny day, a head-high boardshorts session in paradise. There were no tourists for miles. No hotels. No surfers, either. No one had dropped in on Ed all day. He'd been free to ride wave after perfect wave, lost in the purest Dharma imaginable. This is what he'd come to India for. This was surfing a virgin break, alone.

The boisterous shoreline crowd made him feel like a pro at Pipeline, hooting everything he did albeit, if truth be told, Ed had never surfed

Pipe and wouldn't be rushing to do so anytime soon. Initially, though it seemed that their enthusiasm was the mirror image of his, it soon struck Ed that it was impossible for him not to be the more stoked. After all, they were on the beach; he was in the water. And he was the surfer, the one who'd been waiting for waves – since New Year's Eve to be precise. As if to scupper any resolutions to surf more than ever, the swell had dropped overnight, deigning, on 1 January, to serve up no more than waist high, tricky, shallow and fast surf. The pattern continued for over three weeks. Ed knew this place well enough to know that this was to be expected – January is the smallest season – but he was frustrated. There was fun to be had on his fish, and he was finding an awful lot of time to read the Mahabharata, but he needed something more. The surfer in him needed some serious nourishment.

It came in the form of a 3.5-4 ft south-westerly swell with a 14 second period wave, which on this part of the Indian coastline – where Ed had been living for six months – produces a 6-8 ft face on the sets. On flat days, Ed hadn't just read the Mahabharata (the great Sanskrit epic of the Hindus). In fact, he'd been pretty diligent, taking his spluttering Honda Kinetic ZX up and down the coast and noting point, rivermouth and even canal mouth set-ups galore. All it would take would be the right swell and an offshore wind to hold them up. Today, that swell had come and the wind was right. The beach break at Kerala was closing out, but Ed knew that point break perfection was just a few miles away.

Strapping what he liked to call The Green Goddess (a 6 ft 2inch JP quad fish) to his scooter with some frayed coconut rope, Ed arrived at a small fishing hamlet. Swiftly, he untied the Goddess and ran past the mosque to the beach. What he saw amounted to his very own Endless Summer moment. Under a clear blue sky, warmed by the luxuriant Indian morning sun, exquisite left-handers were rumbling into the scimitar-shaped bay, peeling for 200 yards off the headland. A gaggle of local boys were playing in the shallows on the inside; fishermen snoozed in the shade of their boats after a night at sea. Their reverie was interrupted when Ed started to paddle out. What on earth was he doing? Why would anyone want to paddle an odd-looking board out to such ferocious waves? Neither boys nor fishermen had ever seen a surfer before.

Curiosity soon turned to amazement. This strange young man, a 38-year-old graphic designer from Brighton, with a shock of curly blond hair and freckles merging into an even brown thanks to the sun, must be a sorcerer. Time and again he would turn his board, his beloved Green Goddess, toward the shore, jump to his feet and walk on water.

Was that what they thought he was doing? For the first couple of hours – during which his backhand surfing improved out of all recognition – Ed barely gave thought to the meaning of this particular session. The whoops of the onlookers amped him as much as the waves; he was possessed, lost in the sheer physicality of surfing, inwardly exalting that he had an audience. But then it dawned on him – had anyone ever ridden a wave here before? If this was truly a virgin break (and it seemed likely that it was), what on earth were Ed's audience thinking?

He wouldn't be able to ask them. Lost in thought, Ed failed to notice that his fans had left the scene. One minute they were there, the next they were gone, perhaps for lunch or back to school. Again, his mind fell to wondering: was he really the first person to surf this wave? Ed's mind became as insistent as the constant left-handers. *The Surfing Swamis don't mention this place in the guide to surfing in India. It's not in the Stormrider's new guide to surfing in India, either. Maybe a wandering surfer has come through and snagged a few. But then again, maybe not. After all, I've never, ever heard talk of left-hand points like this round here. Is it my discovery?*

If Ed had discovered this spot, shouldn't he to name it? Wasn't that the convention? But if so, how? What does surf lore say about the naming of surf breaks? Was there a code that needed to be followed?

Maybe I could call it 'Ed's Wave'? Or what about 'Ed's Left'? Or maybe 'Templeton's', nice and respectable, Mum and Dad would be pleased.

But then, as he caught his last wave in, Ed had an epiphany. He'd been lost to the ecstasy of a perfect surf, in thrall to the shouts and cheers of the crowd. His ego had taken over. Surfing wasn't about colonization. What did naming a spot matter? Why was it necessary? Wasn't it somehow better not to name this wave, this slice of point break heaven? Otherwise, what was the point of being in India, of reading the Vedas, the Ramayana and the Mahabharata, of practising yoga, pranayama and meditation? Couldn't he – shouldn't he – just call it 'that awesome left point a few miles along the coast'? Or even 'The Spot with No Name'?

It was a quandary all right, and although he surfed that left point for another four days in succession (and thereafter, many times since), Ed has yet to solve it.

LOCO ON LOBOS

Imagine having not only the waves to yourself – but an entire island.

Stef Harkon allowed himself a sly smile. There he was, the only surfer left in the line-up at a world-class but usually ultra-crowded, right-hand point break. He had the place to himself and better yet, the surf was pumping. It had been good all day but now, as everyone else paddled in, it was getting even better.

"What are you doing?" said the last surfer to leave the water, as he paddled past Harkon.

"I'm staying," replied Harkon.

It was no big deal. Harkon had camped overnight on the Canary island of Los Lobos half a dozen times before. Instead of paddling in and walking the 25 minutes to the island's tiny harbour, to catch a ferry back to Fuerteventura at 4pm, he would surf till dusk and then camp overnight on Lobos. This routine meant that he'd be up and surfing at first light, enjoying the surf on his own before the ferry – which left Corralejo daily at 10am – deposited hordes of other surfers on the island.

"See you," said the last surfer in the water as he headed for shore. Harkon watched him paddle in, and then did what he'd come to Lobos for – he surfed his brains out until the light started to fade.

But enjoying the solitude as he was, things didn't go as smoothly as they could have done. The swell had been clean and chest-to-head high all day; as the afternoon wore on, the wind rose, turned onshore and began to mess up the waves. The swell grew, too. By the time Harkon decided to call it a day, he was the last man in 8 ft surf which was far from perfect. The unruly conditions meant that his paddle in didn't go well either. He couldn't reach the usual spot used to get in and out of the sea at Lobos, and ended up being washed down the point, finally coming in over some rocks.

Still, things weren't so bad. Although Harkon's board had picked up a dent, its glassed-in fins were in one piece. He'd cut his shins and knees on the rocks, but not too badly. It was December 1989, the weather was warm and as Harkon made his way across the desert and scrub, back to the lagoon on Lobos where he planned to camp, he thought of his friends, fellow surfers from St Ives who'd decided to stay in Corralejo. They'd be settling down for a few beers in one of the town's bars, but that was fine. Harkon had the uninhabited island of Los Lobos to himself. The surf was up, and would surely be sizable in the morning, but the wind would drop and then he would have some of the best waves on the planet to himself. A few cuts were a small price to pay.

At the lagoon, Harkon settled down for the night. He had a rucksack with the bare essentials for an overnight surf trip: a poncho for warmth, a T-shirt, a pair of boardshorts, a pair of flip-flops, a bottle of water and some cheese and crackers. He also had a Sony Walkman with a pair of large, fluffy orange ear-phones – it was the eighties, after all – and a pair of Speedo swimming trunks. He had just one cassette – an album by The The called 'Infected'. He made what would pass for a camp, ate some cheese and crackers and pressed 'play'. The chorus of the title track diverted his mind:

I can't give you up, till I've got more than enough.
So infect me with your love –
Nurse me into sickness. Nurse me back to health.
Endow me with the gifts – of the man-made world.

After a while, Harkon had had enough of Infected. He found it a touch too dark and angst-ridden. He stopped the cassette and removed his ear-phones. What he heard was astonishing. The surf was booming. Even from the lagoon, some distance from the point break he'd been surfing all day, he could hear massive waves detonating on the rocks. The wind was howling, too. For a moment, he wondered if the sea would settle down by morning, and then, exhausted from the sun and surfing, he went to sleep.

Harkon awoke at dawn. The noise of the sea had entered his dreams, but he'd had a fair night's sleep. Now though, he was worried. If anything, the wind was even more ferocious. He made his way to the harbour, wondering what he would see. The answer was a sea that was out of control. Huge waves were pounding the harbour wall, whipped up into a frenzy by the wind. There was no way Harkon would be surfing today, but something else wouldn't be happening, either. There was no way that the ferry would be coming to Lobos.

Harkon knew that he had another day and night on Lobos ahead of him. Harkon's father, a career soldier, had brought Harkon up to be self-sufficient and capable; the kind of person who wouldn't panic and who could handle difficult situations. Harkon didn't panic, but his father's survival skills did not come to the fore. In fact, Harkon made every mistake in the book.

He decided to top up his tan, and so donned only his Speedos. He decided to do some exercise, and so went for a run around the island. He decided he was hungry, and so ate the last of his food. He decided to go and check out the surf on the point, and so, Infected playing on his Walkman for the umpteenth time, he crossed the scrub and made his way onto the rocks. There, amazed afresh by the size of the surf, up to 12 ft by now, he slipped on the rocks. The Walkman was lost and fresh cuts were sustained. Wearing just his Speedos and, for some unaccountable reason, his fluffy orange ear-phones, Harkon decided to use the last of his water to wash his wounds. By now it was 10am. Harkon returned to the harbour and sat on its wall, scanning the horizon for signs of the ferry. There was nothing.

Harkon spent the day roaming Lobos, staring into space, wondering what to do. He tried using a diver's knife that he'd stowed in his rucksack to catch fish in the lagoon. He spent two hours swimming around, knife in hand, looking for fish – and saw just one. In trying to kill it underwater with a sweeping motion of his right arm, he managed to stab his foot. Later, he wondered if he should try and paddle back to Fuerteventura. It wasn't far, some two kilometres, but the sea was too big. There were sharks, too. It wasn't worth the risk. He resigned himself to seeing out another night on the island.

It was a rough night. He was hungry, dehydrated and shattered from the sun. He thought of his mates, over the water in Corralejo, having a good time. But the thought of them gave him hope. They knew where he was. They wouldn't forget him. Whatever happened, they would come and get him. If they didn't, maybe the school bus would turn up? That was one of his dreams – a vivid, intense, almost hallucinatory dream, the kind that accompany sunstroke or heat exhaustion. His sleep was fitful, and above, in the night sky, the stars seemed to assume abnormal shapes, as if they were mocking the absurd idea of camping for a night on Lobos just to avoid a few fellow surfers in the line-up.

Lobos means 'wolves' in Spanish, the name arising not because untamed members of the Canidae family once roamed the island, but because of the monk seals, or sea wolves, discovered by Spanish conquerors in the fifteenth century. That night Harkon saw, not a wolf of sea or land, but a large white cat. It came towards him and stared, and then wandered off.

Or did it? By morning, ravenous and dehydrated, Harkon couldn't be sure of much. All he knew – *Nurse me into sickness, Nurse me back to health* playing incessantly in his brain even though he'd lost the Walkman – was that he had to get off the island. Awake again at first light, for the third day in succession, he made his way to the point. The sea was still large and choppy, but the swell had subsided a little. Would the ferry come today? He couldn't be sure but decided to make a giant sign spelling 'HELP' on the side of the volcano on Lobos. It was a mad idea. He was too tired. He was all but delirious, and could barely lift the rocks or even spell 'HELP'. He gave up.

But then, joy. Harkon could see the flat-bottomed boat which served as the Corralejo-Lobos ferry bobbing its way to the island. He ran back to the harbour and watched as the captain made an attempt to dock. He failed. The sea was still too rough. Harkon couldn't believe it, surely the captain wasn't going back to Corralejo without him? But yes, he had turned the boat away and was setting off – only to complete a sweep and circle back around.

This time, the captain was able to bring the ferry into the harbour. As soon as it was within range of the harbour wall, Harkon was all action. He grabbed his rucksack and board, took a running jump and leapt onto the boat. He called for water and drank all the way back to Corralejo, where his mates merely said, "Where have you been, then?"

Stef Harkon has since returned many times to surf Los Lobos, but he has never listened to Infected again.

THE LADY IN THE EMERALD GREEN BATHING DRESS

A lawyer's revelations suggest that Agatha Christie may have been on a surf trip when she disappeared for 11 days in December 1926.

Every evening, at 7pm sharp, the Queen of Crime presented herself for dinner in the restaurant of The Swan Hydropathic in Harrogate. According to one of the partners in the discreet and little-known law firm of McNeil & Hodgson, she was always immaculately attired; often, her gown of choice was an emerald green evening dress. "She was unfailingly courteous to the hotel's staff, and yet, for all that she comported herself with poise and decorum, she was also withdrawn, reserved, a woman immersed in her own thoughts," says Peter Robinson, who has been a partner with London-based McNeil & Hodgson for longer than he cares to remember.

"Try as they might, fellow guests were unable to engage the shy and distant thirty-something woman in anything other than a perfunctory chat about the weather," adds Robinson. "No wonder, when you realise why she was there."

Exceptional detective work is not required to ascertain that the Queen of Crime is none other than Agatha Christie, the author of 66 detective novels and 14 short story collections – and the best-selling novelist of all time. Moreover, neither a Hercule Poirot nor a Miss Marple is necessary to deduce that Robinson is referring to Christie's extraordinary disappearance, for a period of 11 days, in December 1926. "She had argued with her husband Archie on the evening of 3 December," confirms Robinson, a softly-spoken man whose healthy frame gives a hint of the steely determination that his clients have come to know and cherish. "Archie was in love with another woman, Nancy Neele, and could no longer contain his feelings. He told Agatha that he wanted a divorce. Theirs was always a tempestuous relationship, so one can only imagine the explosiveness of their row that night. In any event, it resulted in Archie leaving the Berkshire house he shared with Agatha in favour of a weekend in Godalming with his lover. Later that same evening, his wife left the home, too."

Agatha Christie's Morris Cowley car was later found on a slope at Newlands Corner, near Guildford. Already a published author – not least of *The Man in the Brown Suit,* one of Robinson's favourite novels – she left little for a fascinated public to go on: just a letter for her secretary saying that she was going to Yorkshire. Eleven days later, Christie was identified as a guest at the Swan Hydropathic Hotel in Harrogate, Yorkshire. "Rather curiously," says Robinson, "she had registered as 'Mrs Teresa Neele' from Cape Town."

Robinson's discretion is one of the qualities that has seen his niche practice prosper. He is the last man to breach a confidence, but a passion unusual among lawyers sees him relax and open up about his dealings with Christie, who died in 1976. Robinson, like Christie many years before him, is a surfer. And his devotion to surfing means that he has a remarkable theory about what Christie was doing at the Swan Hydropathic for those mysterious 11 days.

"The Swan Hydropathic is now known as The Old Swan," explains Robinson, "but its name and reputation in the 1920s would have been alluring for Christie. She was brought up in South Devon and loved the sea and all things marine. As a young girl she used to take to the water in bathing machines, back in the days when male and female swimming was segregated. She writes in her autobiography of the cumbersome garments she had to wear, of the racier garb of French girls, and of older folks' discontent at the 'progress' that allowed mixed swimming. But despite all the impediments, she says that 'bathing was one of the joys of my life'. It's possible that this was an understatement, but be that as it may, if there's one thing that Agatha Christie loved as much as swimming, it was surfing."

As something of a Christie devotee, both in the sense that his law firm was intimately involved in her affairs and in his enjoyment of her work, Robinson is well-placed to advance a remarkable theory about Christie's motives for her trip to the Swan Hydopathic. "Clearly, she was upset by Archie's liaison with another woman and wanted time out," he says. "A hotel offering hydropathic treatments would have been naturally attractive, given Agatha's lifelong love of bathing, but it's quite possible that she was on a strange kind of surf trip – Harrogate is a spa town, but it's not actually on the coast."

Anyone hearing such an assertion might be tempted to conclude that Robinson has gone slightly mad but he insists, with the conviction of Poirot, Christie's most infamous sleuth, that the clues stack up. "You just need to read *The Man in the Brown Suit*, and then Christie's autobiography," avows Robinson. "Then add a few contextual elements. It's more than likely that rather than being in a state of fugue for those 11 days, as Andrew Norman suggests in *The Finished Portrait* (his account of the disappearance), Christie was seeking to recapture memories of surfing and contemplating a trip to the Yorkshire coast in search of waves."

The Man in the Brown Suit yields references to Muizenberg, a beachside suburb of Cape Town, South Africa. Christie's heroine, Anne Beddingfield, embarks on an investigative odyssey which takes her from London to South Africa, where she enters a world of diamond thieves, murderers and political intrigue. Classic Christie, but not so what happens on Beddingfield's trip to Muizenberg, a journey she takes by way of recreational relief. The intrepid young woman goes surfing:

"Surfing looks perfectly easy. It isn't. I say no more. I got very angry and fairly hurled my plank from me. Nevertheless, I determined to return on the first possible opportunity and have another go. Quite by mistake I then got a good run on my board and came out delirious with happiness. Surfing is like that. You are either vigorously cursing or else you are idiotically pleased with yourself."

Robinson explains that Beddingfield's narration has its exact counterpart in Christie's life. "In January 1922, she set off on a world tour with Archie. He had been asked to join a trade delegation to promote a British Empire Exhibition that would be held in London in 1924. Over the course of the year they visited South Africa, Australia, New Zealand and Canada, ending up in Hawaii. Christie first went surfing in South Africa, where she would lie prone on her board and ride waves to the shore, but it was at Waikiki that she really mastered the art."

And so, thanks to Christie's autobiography, it proves. She and Archie arrived in Honolulu, Oahu on 5 August 1922. As soon as they had checked in, they went surfing. "We arrived in the early morning, got into our rooms at the hotel and straight away, seeing out of the window the people surfing on the beach, we rushed down, hired our surf-boards, and plunged into the sea."

The couple's efforts were not initially successful. "We were complete innocents," writes Christie. She and Archie were regularly "flung asunder" from boards that they found to be much heavier than those on which they had proned to the shore at Muizenberg, and "a catastrophe" occurred when Christie's "handsome silk bathing dress, covering me from shoulder to ankle was more or less torn from me by the force of the waves." Almost nude, she made for her beach wrap and then visited the hotel shop where she bought "a wonderful, skimpy, emerald green wool bathing dress, which was the joy of my life, and in which I thought I looked remarkably well. Archie thought I did too."

In taking to Waikiki's waves Christie and her husband were following in illustrious British footsteps. Research by Pete Robinson, the man at the helm of the Museum of British Surfing, has revealed that in 1920, Edward Prince of Wales went surfing. "On his first trip to Waikiki in

April 1920 he was taken out in an outrigger canoe, then later in the day was coaxed into standing up on a surfboard to ride the waves for the first time, by the great Olympian and father of modern surfing, Duke Kahanamoku," says Robinson. He adds that "The future King Edward VIII was so stoked on surfing that he ordered his royal ship HMS Renown to return for three days in September just to surf! On this secret surf trip he hooked up with Duke's brother David Kahanamoku, and along with his great friend Lord Louis Mountbatten, they went surfing every day."

There is photographic evidence of Prince Edward's surf skills, and there is ample written evidence of Christie's surfing at Waikiki's gentle reef breaks, the likes of Populars, Queens and Canoes. "All our days were spent on the beach and surfing, and little by little we learned to become expert, or at any rate expert from the European point of view. We cut our feet to ribbons on the coral until we bought ourselves soft leather boots to lace round our ankles."

But what of the legal eagle Robinson and his claim that Christie's trip to Harrogate was in some way connected to surfing?

"From their arrival in early August to their departure in October, the Christies did little but surf," says Robinson. "Agatha wrote that surfing was 'heaven' and 'one of the most perfect physical pleasures' she had ever known. She was wholly enamoured of what, for the Hawaiians, has always been the sport of kings and given that she immersed herself so much in surfing, it's reasonable to infer that she would have been told of the two Hawaiian princes who went surfing in Bridlington in 1890."

The young men to whom Robinson refers were Prince Jonah Kuhio Kalanianaole Piikoi and his brother Prince David Kahalepouli Kawananakoa Piikoi, who were taken on holiday to Bridlington by their English guardian as a reward for studying hard. A letter in the archives of the Bishop Museum in Honolulu sees Kuhio declare "We enjoy the seaside very much and are out swimming every day. The weather has been very windy these few days and we like it very much, for we like the sea to be rough so that we are able to have surf riding. We enjoy surf riding very much and surprise the people to see us riding on the surf."

Bridlington is 67 miles from Harrogate. Could it be that Christie took herself to the Swan Hydropathic Hotel with a view to making a further trip to the Yorkshire coast, where she would simultaneously emulate the example of the Hawaiian princes and reacquaint herself with the joy of surfing?

"Yes," says Robinson, from deep inside the offices of McNeil & Hodgson. "The clues are plain to see. This was a woman who adored surfing, and whose happiest moments with her difficult husband had been when they were surfing. I don't think she was in a trance, unaware of her actions, when she took herself to the Swan Hydropathic, as has been alleged. It seems to me that the evidence is clear. Agatha Christie was on a surf trip. She was desperate both to recapture what proved to be lost moments of happiness – she and Archie divorced in 1928 – and simply to enjoy the cleansing sensation of the sea and surfing again. It was a surf trip that was only scuppered when she was recognised by a fellow guest at the hotel."

It is a claim that may yet illumine Christie's 11-day disappearance thanks to ongoing research by Robinson's namesake and his assistant, Felicity Lemon, at the Museum of British Surfing.

"As with so much of surfing history, not just in Britain but around the world," he says, with an enigmatic smile, "there is more than meets the eye. Was the lady who loved her emerald green bathing dress planning to go surfing at Bridlington? I wouldn't bet against it."

PURRING THANKS TO 'DA CAT'

Surfers the world over were touched by Californian legend Miki Dora.

"Miki Dora was probably the purest surfer who ever waxed a board. He had a style that was completely his own. He was remarkable."

The man who succinctly articulated what Hungary-born, California-raised Miki Dora meant to surfing is Greg Noll, otherwise known as 'Da Bull'. Noll is no less deserving of acclaim on account of pioneering big wave riding exploits in the 1960s at places like Makaha, Waimea Bay and Pipeline. Of one 25 ft wave at Outside Pipeline, Noll wrote: "Instead of getting smaller as I rode it, the sonofabitch grew on me. It got bigger and bigger, and I started going faster and faster, until I was absolutely locked into it. I felt like I was on a spaceship racing into a void."

For many people, dealing with Dora was not so much like racing into a void but slipping into one unawares. Born in Budapest in 1934, he was an enigma all the way through his life until his death in 2002 from pancreatic cancer. He was notoriously elusive, cryptic on the rare occasions he gave interviews, and when surfing, as iconoclastic as he was effortlessly elegant. The two qualities came together at the right-hand point break of Malibu, the surf break synonymous with Dora, in its 1967 Invitational Surf Classic. In what was to be his last contest, Dora caught a wave, leapt as nimbly as ever to his feet and trimmed smoothly across its face until he passed in front of the judges. He then dropped his trademark black shorts and bent over, lending physical, visceral expression to his castigation of competition judges as "senile surf freaks".

But whatever his flaws – and Dora had them in spades, serving terms of imprisonment for credit card fraud and becoming renowned for both his unreliability and paradoxical nature (he professed to loathe the 1960s' commercialisation of surfing, but was happy enough to make money as a stunt double in surf exploitation movies like *Ride the Wild Surf* and *Beach Party)* – his surfing ability was never in doubt. This, allied with handsome looks, a fine physique and oodles of charisma, led to a soubriquet which was the antithesis of Noll's. The big and muscular Noll was 'Da Bull'; Dora, also big and muscular but ineffably light on his feet, was 'Da Cat'.

In the way he lived his life and the style which he brought to riding waves, Dora was surfing's answer to Jack Kerouac. An outlaw who refused to answer to anyone's rules or, as *The Times* put it in his obituary, a "West Coast archetype and antihero . . . the siren voice of a nonconformist surfing lifestyle." And like all outlaws, Dora left an indelible mark on all who met him – whether he meant to or not.

Mike Newman, a Cornwall-based photographer, met Da Cat while surfing at Jeffrey's Bay in South Africa in 1997. "I'd spent the summer teaching surfing at Sennen Cove and headed off in September on a surf trip that ended up lasting a year," recalls Newman, who travelled with Kirstin Gorvin, one of west Cornwall's best surfers. The pair spent three months in South Africa, where they encountered tragedy as much as elation.

The former came when they met up with Clyde Crawford, a Sydney-based physiotherapist and surfer. "Clyde is a good friend and I was stoked to see him," says Newman, "but he had a terrible tale to tell.

He told us that he was suiting up with a mate to go and surf Breezy Point, a break on the Wild Coast, near Umtata. The pair had surfed the point all morning with a friend called Mark Penches, who was also from Sydney. They'd come in for lunch and were getting changed to head out for an afternoon surf. They entered the water and Mark was ahead of them, keen for more waves. Clyde said that Mark paddled about 200 yards to the line-up and had just taken off on his first wave, when his board suddenly disappeared. Then they heard screams and a woman shouting 'Shark! Shark!' There was nothing they could do."

Within half an hour, one of Penches's arms was washed onto the beach; later, the remains of a leg, with surfboard leash still attached, came ashore. Crawford had to walk two miles to find the nearest phone and call for help, and had to repatriate Penches's remains to Australia.

"There were sharks at so many breaks," says Newman. "We'd turn up somewhere and find perfect, lined-up sets reeling across reefs and points – and no one out. The reason was always the same: a Great White or some other kind of shark had been spotted." Experts reckoned that Penches was taken by a Great White, a Tiger or a Zambezi (also known as a Bull) shark, all common to the rugged Wild Coast of South Africa's Eastern Cape.

But although sharks were a problem, South Africa boasts a number of world class breaks – none better than Jeffrey's Bay, which is widely regarded as the best right-hand point break on the planet. Newman and Gorvin, both natural footers, were in seventh heaven, not least because it was, as Newman recalls, "an *El Niño* year. You normally need a 3.2 mm wetsuit for J-Bay but it was so unusually warm that there were plenty of times when we could surf in boardshorts."

One session has lingered in Newman's mind for the best part of two decades. "It was about 6-8 ft, clean and perfect. There were only about 10 people in the line up. J-Bay is a classic wave. You can ride it for at least 300 yards, carving huge turns, getting barrelled and going faster than just about anywhere else – and I had one of the rides of my life. I took off, got the line just right and screamed along, carving and hitting the lip and getting a cover up or two, and topped it all with my exit." This may sound strange, but Newman is not referring to an exceptionally brilliant kick-out. "At J-Bay there are various different sections. Each section of the wave has a different name, although it's the same wave running along the edge of the same bay. I was surfing Super Tubes. There's a reef right in front of the beach, and it has a keyhole, a cut of sand that makes for an easy way back to the beach, one that doesn't destroy your fins or mean that your feet are cut to shreds on the mussel-covered reef. I could see the keyhole looming as I was hammering down the line, and managed to prone through it and paddle in to the beach. It all came together smoothly and I was pretty pleased with it. I admit it, I thought that the ride and the exit, taken together, made for one of those surfing experiences that I wished someone had seen."

Back on the sand, Newman stood with his board under his arm, looking back at a perfect J-Bay. Just then, a man on his way to Super Tubes walked past with a plain, white 8 ft board. He had greying hair, looked to be in his early sixties and had a slight paunch. "As he passed me, kind of cruising along, he looked at me and said 'A guy's gotta be pleased with a wave like that.' I was, and I was stoked too, that someone had seen it after all."

But Newman was yet more elevated when someone else on the beach told him that the compliment had been paid by none other than Miki 'Da Cat' Dora.

"I couldn't believe it," he says. "It's always nice if someone sees your best waves, but when that someone is Miki Dora – and he says you've just surfed well – it doesn't get much better than that, does it?"

In some ways, it didn't: for the remainder of Newman and Gorvin's time at J-Bay, Dora's remark on the beach was as civil as he got. "He would drop in on absolutely everyone," says Newman, chuckling. "He just didn't care. But even though he had a slightly hunched style – he wasn't really ''Da Cat' by then – he would always get the longest rides."

Newman's year-long surf trip later saw him meet Nat Young, the Australian surfer who was world champion in 1966. Newman was talking to Young at his home in Angourie, New South Wales, and told him of Dora's ruthlessness in the line up at Jeffrey's Bay. It would not have been a revelation – at Malibu, Dora was renowned for pushing people off boards or running them over if they got in his way – and Young was indulgent. "I guess he's earned the right to be like that by now," said Young.

In 2000, Young – whose nickname in his prime was 'The Animal' – was the victim of a severe beating following an incident of surf rage. "He'd berated a grom for what he called 'bad behaviour', slapping his face, only to find the kid's dad waiting on the beach," says Newman. The incident, which left Young with shattered cheekbones and broken eye sockets, caused him to re-evaluate his attitude to other surfers. He admitted he had acted aggressively in his past and co-authored a book entitled *Surf Rage* which called for greater tolerance in the surfing community.

By the time of Young's Damascene conversion, Miki 'Da Cat' Dora was in his mid-sixties. Less than two years later, on 3 January 2002, Dora died at his father's home in Montecito, California. Somehow, it seems unlikely that he repented his arrogant ways in the water, but the curious thing about 'Da Cat' – who once said "Life's a waste of time, and surfing is as good a way to waste it as any" – is that it doesn't matter whether he did or not. As Mike Newman can testify, and thousands of other surfers will agree, Da Cat made people purr. Or, as Young's autobiography has it, 'Nat's Nat, And That's That'.

PART SEVEN

Obsession

PEG LEG RIK

Rik Bennett is a chef with one leg who runs the fish shop in St Agnes. But most of all, he's a surfer.

Everyone who surfs knows that it is one of the most difficult sports to learn. It's not like football, rugby or athletics; it's not even like skiing, snowboarding or many of the other so-called 'extreme' sports. The key reason for the difference is that, in surfing, the surfer is dealing with a constantly moving substance, rather than a static and stable environment. The sea moves. No one wave is ever the same as the last. Minute variables occur, making for fractional adjustments and split-second decision-making. Add the need for decent upper body strength, a good pair of lungs and a reasonable degree of natural agility, and the beginner soon realises that the basics of say, football, are a lot easier than those of surfing.

But how much more difficult is surfing if you only have one leg? Surely, then, surfing is impossible? Of course, waves can still be ridden, but only prone, on a bodyboard or bellyboard, or sitting in a waveski or sea kayak. To stand up and ride a wave minus a limb must be beyond the will of man.

Wrong. There is a surfer in the Cornish village of St Agnes who proves that where there is a will, there is a way. That man is Rik Bennett. For a time, he ran a fish shop and deli in St Agnes. But he's not known as Rik, or Riky, or Richard. Everyone calls him 'Peg Leg' for one very simple reason: he only has one leg. And remarkably, Peg Leg Rik – to give him the long form of his name – is a very good surfer.

"Peg Leg, now he's a phenomenon," says Peter 'Chops' Lascelles, an Australian émigré who runs Beachbeat Surfboards in St Agnes. Chops is a former Queensland surfing champion, and has established Beachbeat as one of the foremost surf shops (complete with a cutting edge board shaping facility), in Europe. When it comes to surfing, he knows his stuff. "Peg Leg is an amazing guy. He's probably the most stoked surfer I know. He's a good longboarder and I'm proud to have him on the Beachbeat team as a board tester."

Peg Leg Rik was born without an ankle on his left leg. His parents took medical advice about how to give their son the best quality of life possible. "The surgeon told them they had two options," says Rik. "I could have the lower part of my left leg surgically removed, or I could wear a big club shoe for the rest of my life. Mum and Dad asked him what he'd do if he was in their place. He said he'd have the leg removed, so that, with their consent, is what happened."

As a child, Rik was a water baby. He says that a holiday to Perranporth, another Cornish surfing stronghold, was a turning point in his life. "I came to Perranporth to see some friends in 1985, and just ended up staying. I learnt to surf almost as soon as I arrived, thanks to local surfers like Rob Small, Mark Thorn and John Hudson. I had a prosthetic leg but it wasn't one that I could take into the water, so I had to learn with just one leg. Initially I went bodyboarding, but got bored of it after six months, and moved onto a kneeboard. It was super fast and more fun, but after a while I just thought 'Sod it, I want to stand up'. The guys had me paddling out in 6 ft waves before I'd figured out how to pop-up, but soon enough I was standing up, albeit with a bit of a strange style."

By then, surfing was in Rik's blood. He kept at it, paddling out in all conditions, getting stronger and better all the time. Then came another turning point. "I managed to get a prosthetic 'beach activities' leg from the National Health Service. It made an immediate difference, giving me lots more manoeuvrability. Before I acquired the new leg, I had no way of readjusting my position, but now I could cross-step to the nose and do decent bottom turns with more drive. Over time, I figured out that I needed to drill small holes into the leg to relieve the pressure that would build up during surfs."

Eight years after he first stood up and rode a wave, Rik discovered his favourite wave – Lakey Peak in Sumbawa, Indonesia. "In 1993 I went travelling in Indonesia for 18 months," he says. "It was my first proper surf trip and I went all over the place, living pretty rough. Lakey Peak was just a gem of a find. I love having the choice to go left or right."

Nearby Lakey Peak, a reef break which offers left and right-handers, is Nungas, a left-hander. Here Rik nearly lost his leg. "I paddled out into the biggest waves I'd ever seen with two Aussie surfers. They were calling it a solid 15 ft, but they were pretty good surfers from Margaret River and for me, the surf was touching 20 ft. I ended up getting eaten on this one wave. My leash snapped and I lost my board, then ended up swirling around on the inside in the rip. I thought that was it for me, the end, but I made it onto the reef – with my leg still attached."

But at another one of Indonesia's world class waves – the left-hander known as Uluwatu, in Bali – Rik did lose his leg. "I pulled into a barrel but didn't make it out. When I came up, the leg was floating next to me, there on the surface. That's when I found out that it floats. Thank God. If I'd lost it, my surf trip would have been over and I probably wouldn't have made it out of the cove. I just bear-hugged my leg and let myself get washed into the reef. I got quite a few funny looks."

Rik spent 25 years working as a chef in Cornwall, surfing his home break of St Agnes and hi-tailing it to Indonesia whenever he could. He now works as a postman in Perranporth, and insists that everything he has achieved is down to his wife Sally and their children, Elfie, Pollyanna, Bluebell Elowen and Finley.

Another of St Agnes' surfing sons, Rip Curl's James Hendy, is as effusive as Lascelles when talking about 'Peg Leg': "Rik rips. He goes out in anything and nothing will stop him surfing. If he's not in Cornwall he'll be in Indo, at Lakey Peak, doing what he loves."

Rik has a clothes peg stencilled onto his red longboard, with the word 'Ebilgarr' underneath. It means 'peg leg' in Cornish, and as he says, "I can't see myself stopping surfing any time soon. I always thought my surfing life would be over by the time I hit 30, maybe 35, because of problems with the knee. But I'm in my forties now and I'm still going strong. Even when I'm 70 I'll be down there on my wooden bellyboard. If I can't get in the ocean, that's it, I'm over, done.

"I do it because it makes me who I am: Peg, the surfer."

SOLDIERS GET STOKED

A pioneering social enterprise group is bringing joy to former servicemen – by taking them surfing.

'Being stoked' is the surfer's preferred condition. It comes of riding good surf, being in the sea, chatting to friends while waiting for waves and seeing marine life such as seabirds, seals and dolphins. It's the converse of how servicemen feel in war zones, as Rich Emerson knows only too well. At the age of 22, he joined the Queen's Royal Irish Hussars and served in Operation Desert Storm. Following this, he spent years suffering from a condition barely even recognised 20 years ago: Post-Traumatic Stress Disorder (PTSD).

"I'd have nightmares about Kuwait, about burning oil fields and the terrible things I saw there," says Emerson. "I'd have a horrible, almost constant state of anxiety and would get into a self-destructive spiral of drinking, suicidal thoughts and depression. But I didn't know anything about PTSD. Nor did anyone around me."

An excellent sportsman from an early age, Emerson emulated his father (a Royal Marines Colour Sergeant) and became a PTI (Physical

Training Instructor). He became the Army Single Sculling Champion and also boxed for his regiment and he is unhesitating when says: "I was proud to serve my country and to help in the liberation of Kuwait. I loved being in the army, experiencing its camaraderie and sense of purpose."

But after he left in 1993, Emerson's life unravelled. Emerson was 27 and had been married to Katherine, with whom he had four children, Victoria, Luke, Nathaniel and Elizabeth. But his increasingly erratic behaviour contributed to his divorce – not once, but twice. His second marriage, to Carol, also foundered, but only later, when he was diagnosed as suffering from PTSD, did Emerson understand why.

Emerson today is softly spoken and calm, with blue eyes that are bright and alert. Tattoos betray his military past, his children and his sporting accomplishments. And a weathered, tanned face hints at how Emerson made the first steps to getting his life back on track.

"I started surfing when I was 30," he says. Emerson was visiting Cornwall to see his first wife and children. He encountered solid, 4 ft surf at St Ives' Porthmeor Beach. "I was with a mate and I just looked at the surfers and said to him 'That's what I want to do'." Emerson acted on impulse, buying a board and wetsuit and learning to surf when he returned to Bournemouth and West Wittering, where he was then living. But before long, he had moved to Cornwall. Becoming a surfer helped him deal with the difficulties of his second marriage breaking up – "I've been very lucky, the surfing community has been brilliant to me," he says – and gave him a newfound sense of purpose. Then came another turning point.

"I got a lot of help from my partner Emma, who contacted the British Legion on my behalf," says Emerson. "Through them, I was introduced to the Warrior Programme, a charity designed to help ex-servicemen. Then I attended Operation Amped in California." At this point, Emerson's eyes light up, as if the burning oil fields of Kuwait have at last left his memory. "Operation Amped was set up in 2006 to introduce American servicemen to surfing. The reason? Surfing can change your life."

Emerson relished his experience with Operation Amped, and returned to Britain with a mission: he would help other combat veterans discover the unique sense of renewal that comes from surfing.

Along with surfer and photographer Russ Pierre, Emerson set up Surf Action, a social enterprise group which, like Operation Amped, is dedicated to improving the lives of veterans suffering from PTSD or physical injuries from their experience of conflict. Surf Action has gone on to become hugely respected in the UK, with the group's instructors often to be seen taking former servicemen surfing on British beaches.

One event, 'Operation Cornish Wave', saw members of Hasler Company, a newly formed rehabilitation unit of the Royal Marines, take to the sea at Polzeath, north Cornwall. "It was a humbling and emotional experience to see amputees and veterans suffering from PTSD riding waves," says Pierre. "To many people the images we see on television, of Afghanistan or other conflicts, have little impact, but to put a name and a face to the brave young men we know are being injured – and to then see them achieve something great, to see the smiles and laughter – is hugely inspirational."

Among the soldiers stoked by Operation Cornish Wave were Nicholas 'Gibbo' Gibbons, a young man who served with 45 Commando in Afghanistan, and Jason Hare, in his mid-forties and also from 45 Commando. Both had suffered terribly, but, says Pierre, described their experience of surfing as "hoofing" and "awesome". Likewise, Trevor Luttrell, a man in his sixties who still suffers from occasional episodes of PTSD after a lifelong military career who says: "It's a magic moment when you're borne along by a wave and it's wonderful for your self-confidence."

But perhaps Emerson himself remains Surf Action's most compelling case history. With tangible relief, he says that PTSD no longer troubles him. There may yet be one or two wobbles, but the nightmares have gone. The anger, guilt and depression are at bay. He credits the well-respected charity Talking to Minds, which specialises in helping veterans with PTSD overcome their problems, with helping him, so too his experience of Neuro-Linguistic Programming techniques. But anyone who surfs will know that surfing has also played a huge part in Emerson's transformation.

The old tagline has it that 'Only a surfer knows the feeling'; it may be that a combat surfer knows that feeling better than anyone else.

THE DAILY WAVESTER

Dale Webster has surfed every day for over 35 years. Stoked, yes – but is he also a bit mad?

Bodega Bay, a rocky inlet some 40 miles north of San Francisco, took Alfred Hitchcock's fancy in 1961. Having decided to adapt Daphne du Maurier's 1952 novella *The Birds,* which sees a British farming family attacked by a variety of kamikaze birds, the director was keen on transposing it to an American coastal location. The prevailing fog, stark surrounding landscape and sense of isolation at Bodega Bay appealed to Hitchcock, who soon returned to film what the movie's 1963 tagline billed as "the most terrifying motion picture I have ever made".

Dale Webster was 15 when *The Birds* was released. By then he was in thrall to surfing, but time at the beach was only possible if he had ticked off chores set by his parents. "My parents gave me the personal freedom to be a surfer," says Dale – but the freedom came at a price. "It was almost a way to control me I guess. 'You can't go to the beach until you clean your room, take out the trash, clean the dishes,' they'd tell me."

One day in 1975, 12 years after Hitchcock's psycho-thriller hit the screens, Dale Webster went for a surf. Nothing odd about that: after all, he was surfer. But on 2 September 1975, something happened to Dale. Or rather, something happened the following day, on 3 September, when a storm hit the beaches of Sonoma County in Northern California. What happened was that Dale went for a surf. He went the next day and the next day, and the day after. Every day, day after day, he went for a surf until at some point, a goal crystallised: Dale would go for a surf every day and catch a minimum of three waves to the beach.

The setting for this quest was Bodega Bay, deemed perfect by Hitchcock for a psychological horror story. Which makes for the greater number – showings of *The Birds* or waves ridden by Webster? The eccentric surfer may just have the edge: he has made it into the Guinness Book of Records and has surfed for over 13,000 consecutive days.

The genesis of so Quixotic a venture is unclear. At times, Dale calls it simply "an incredible excuse to get stoked". He's also on record as having "misread" various signs, all of which apparently propelled him into the sea. They include erroneously believing he needed to surf every day for a year for the repair warranty on his wetsuit to be valid, and trying to beat what he thought was the record for the most consecutive days surfed (5,280), only to find that this was actually the record (in feet) for the longest distance surfed to shore. Similarly, at one stage when deciding to surf for the duration of a lunar cycle, he admits that he misunderstood how long a lunar cycle actually was. As Dale put it, in an interview with *Surfing* magazine: "Did you ever hear of a pilot named Douglas 'Wrong Way' Corrigan back in the thirties? He made his flight plans for California and he landed in Europe. And that's basically what I've done; I've misread all these different things."

Along the way, Dale – who lives eight miles from the ocean in the quiet village of Valley Ford – has gone through just over an average of a wetsuit a year and scooped off roughly the weight of a small child in board wax. He has seen sharks, one of which was a great white; surfed through hail, hurricanes and the pain of kidney stones; and somehow made it to the beach even when his car has broken down. He got married to Kaye; raised a daughter, Margo; never travelled to see Kaye's parents (who lived in Utah); and somehow kept surfing even as he tended Kaye through blood cancer, from which she ultimately died. All this, to ride three waves a day in water that isn't exactly warm: some ten degrees centigrade on a good day.

Daughter Margo surfs too, but that isn't the only way she chose to emulate her father. Margo never missed a day of school, all the way from kindergarten to the end of high school. Dale is proud of her. "I'm so stoked for her, she can do whatever she wants; she doesn't have to live her life locked in like I am," he told *Surfing.*

But Dale's routine isn't one of fun all the way. He laments the way surfing has evolved, complaining about "more and more of these moulded, third-world boards" and what he calls "leaping lizard, splash dancing, whoopdy-whoo surfing". People who don't ride a wave to its conclusion, kicking out in control, prompt his ire; so too having to share waves with people who don't have the same share-and-share-alike attitude: "I have to keep away from people who won't keep away from *me*. They paddle right up next to you and catch the wave you were waiting for. It's just no rules, no respect, free-for-all surfing."

All of the above, as well as having finally surfed for the duration of a lunar cycle (28 years), prompted Dale to declare that he was quitting in 2004. He didn't. He hinted at stopping again in 2009, when he reached 33 years of consecutive surfing. Again, the day came and was followed by another day – and so Dale continued surfing.

A key motivation throughout has been wanting to be acknowledged as a surfer. In fact, Dale wants to be on the cover of *Surfer* magazine. "I wanted people to think of me, to see me, to realize that I'm a surfer. And back in those days [growing up as a surfer in California] *Surfer* magazine was considered the bible of the sport. My dream is still to make the cover of the bible of the sport. And if I don't? For a surfer to surf religiously and not make the bible of the sport? Then as far as I'm concerned, *Surfer* magazine won't be able to call itself the bible of the sport anymore."

Chances are, as you read this, Dale Webster has just been for a surf, or is just about to go for a surf. Or he may even be riding a wave.

And maybe, somewhere in the world, someone is watching *The Birds*, Hitchcock's film of the Du Maurier story in which symbols of peace mutate into a hostile, threatening menace. It's certain that neither Hitchcock nor *The Birds* will ever make it onto the cover of *Surfer*; what's not clear is whether Dale's quest to get there is a thing of beauty, or horror.

THE AMAZING MR SLATER

Hail Mary, it's the man from Cocoa Beach. But who else?

A 5 ft 9 inch, muscular, shaven-headed surfer is riding frontside at speed on a clean, 6 ft wave. In a split second he hits the breaking lip of the wave. He doesn't slash it and go for a conventional 180 degree turn. Instead, he flies up into the air. In a blur his white board is angled way beyond the exploding white water. Extraordinarily, the red-vested surfer proceeds to spin 360 degrees in the air, plunging some 10 feet before landing in front of the close-out wave. For a moment, it seems that he may have fallen, but no – he is merely obscured in the spray. The man is still standing, still surfing.

The man is 40-year-old Kelly Slater, 11 times the surfing world champion. In the words of Australian surfer Josh Kerr – one of the best in the world when it comes to aerial manoeuvres – Slater has just performed "one of the biggest no-grab, to-the-flat, full-rotations ever seen".

Yet more amazingly, Slater has pulled off the move in the middle of a contest – specifically, the final of the 2012 Rip Curl Pro Bells Beach. Today's surf magazines and films are full of surfers flying through the air, executing above-the-lip trickery that could barely have been dreamt of 50 years ago, but often enough, the images are from free surfing sessions, when the pressure is off. Not so when it comes to Slater. As Kerr went on to tell Australia's Stab magazine, "He's a proper, ridiculous sportsman, because he rises above even his own level when he's in the heat of competition."

For Kerr, only Slater could have conceived of so massive a frontside full rotation – an ankle-breaker if ever there was one – in the midst of a contest. No wonder the move is known as a Hail Mary.

"He had a long way down," said Kerr. "But he knew exactly what he was doing."

A familiar staple of the sports pages is the list of the world's greatest sportsmen and women. It's always guaranteed to generate debate, albeit that the same names occur time and again. They include seven time world champion Michael Schumacher, widely regarded as one of the greatest racing drivers of all time, and, on two rather less environmentally unfriendly wheels, Lance Armstrong, who survived testicular cancer to win the Tour de France a record seven consecutive times. Another oft-seen name is Tiger Woods. Whatever the troubles in his personal life, nothing will ever detract from the fact that Woods was the world number one golfer for the most consecutive weeks. Woods was also the PGA Player of the Year a record 10 times.

Other names to conjure with range from Muhammad Ali, Joe Louis and Sugar Ray Leonard to Pele, George Best, Maradona and Johann Cruyff, to McEnroe, Borg and Navratilova and Federer, Sampras and the Williams sisters, all the way to Michael Jordan, Paula Radcliffe and Usain Bolt.

But absurdly – ridiculously – lists of the world's greatest sportspeople perennially omit Kelly Slater. The omission is inconceivable. There is no doubt whatsoever that Slater is not just an exceptional surfer, he is also one of the most exceptional athletes the world has ever seen.

* * *

It's the final of the 2012 Rip Curl Pro Bells Beach. There's a nice cheque for the winner – $75,000 – and the famous beach is packed with spectators eager to see who will take home the spoils. It's the second event of the 2012 World Tour; the first, the Quiksilver Pro presented by Land Rover, was held a few weeks earlier on the Gold Coast. Seasoned pro Taj Burrow won the event, but he won't be celebrating victory this time; the finals pit Slater against yet another Aussie hotshot, the 2007 and 2009 world champion, Mick 'White Lightning' Fanning.

Time and again Slater and Fanning up the ante, exchanging the lead several times with a series of high-scoring waves. Fanning's sweeping carves echo the lines drawn at Bells by the power surfers of yesteryear. However, he has more speed and manages more moves and turns than even the likes of the late Michael Peterson – three times a winner at Bells – and adds a few aerials too, including a remarkable double-tap to lien. Slater's approach is different. While Fanning is wowing the judges with what he was doing *on* the faces of the waves, Slater decides to show what could be done *above* them. The result is the massive, no hands, 360-degree rotation that so impresses Kerr – and everyone in surfing – as well as another air and a carving 360-turn in the lip of a wave.

The final at Bells Beach on 6 April 2012 goes down in history as one of the best man-on-man surf contests ever. Interviewed by Drew Kampion, an influential writer in the world of surf journalism, Slater once said "My belief is that heaven and hell are metaphorical terms for what you make of your life. In any instant, you have the ability to make your life total pleasure or total hell."

Slater has done a very good job of bringing total pleasure to everyone who loves surfing. His unparalleled career in professional surfing demonstrates both preternatural athleticism and an extraordinary ability, over countless instants, to make the right decision, in the right place, at the right time.

Robert Kelly Slater is, quite simply, the greatest surfer ever. Born in Cocoa Beach, Florida on 11 February 1972, Slater is both the youngest surfer ever to win the ASP world title, and the oldest. He was first crowned champion in 1992 at the age of 20, and has gone on to be crowned a further 10 times, winning the eleventh championship in 2011 at the age of 40.

The records don't stop there. In pro surfing, in each heat the ASP operates a two-wave scoring system in which a surfer's best two waves are aggregated, with a maximum possible score of 20 (10 points being the maximum for each wave); needless to say, Slater is the first surfer ever to score a perfect 20 (in May 2005, in the final heat of the Billabong Tahiti Pro contest at Teahupoo). He easily outpaces Australian surfer Mark Richards' four ASP titles (the previous record until Slater came along), and has the highest number of World Championship Tour contest wins in surfing history (48 and counting). For the surfing cognoscenti, Hawaii remains the proving ground, but here too, Slater has excelled, winning the most prestigious individual event on the WCT, the Pipeline Masters, a record five times.

Slater's celebrity status has been enhanced by high-profile romances with Cameron Diaz (herself a surfer), Pamela Anderson and Brazilian supermodel Gisele Bundchen. He appeared in several episodes of *Baywatch* in the early 1990s and, a talented guitarist, he has also performed with Ben Harper and Pearl Jam. Inevitably, there is a hugely successful video game too – the aptly named Kelly Slater's Pro Surfer – not to mention endless starring roles in surf movies, perhaps the most famous of which is the Jack Johnson showcase, *Thicker Than Water.*

It's all a far cry from his early years at Cocoa Beach, where Slater's parents, Steve and Judy, experienced debilitating financial problems. The couple divorced when their middle son was 11 (Slater's brothers, Sean and Steven, are also excellent surfers). The boys witnessed their father's uneasy relationship with alcohol, and perhaps, as with so many high achievers, a degree of parental dysfunction contributed to Slater's immense drive. That drive, in turn, has taken him to a wealthy lifestyle which he could never have imagined as a young boy, but his success is fundamentally down to a freakish natural talent in the sea. To watch Slater surf is to be mesmerized by a blend of suppleness, power and elegance allied with an uncanny wave-reading skill. His surfing is so fluid and gymnastic that it's as if he inhabits the ocean, rather than merely visits it.

Like his childhood hero and three-times world champion Tom Curren, Slater on land is no less notable. Both walk with a feline grace – a nuanced, barely discernible, but subtle awareness of everything in their environment. It's a rare thing, and what's more, Slater knows it. As he says, "Most anything I've ever set my mind to, I could accomplish. I felt like I was always in the right place at the right time."

* * *

Bells Beach, 6 April 2012. Slater has just landed his Hail Mary rotation. The judges give him a perfect 10. Fanning has earlier posted a 9.1; he responds to Slater's extraordinary aerial with a 9.7. Slater needs another huge wave to edge ahead and clinch the 40-minute final. If anyone can do it, it's him, but it's not to be. He scores well but not well enough; Fanning bags his first victory at Bells since he won as a teenage wildcard in 2001.

Slater takes home $30,000 for his second place finish. His career earnings now stand at over $3 million. With hundreds of thousands of dollars also netted from sponsorship deals, books, TV and media appearances, Slater is comfortably a multi-millionaire.

But Slater remains down-to-earth and approachable. He may be possessed by a competitive drive of terrifying, not to mention age-defying proportions, but there are many tales of average, everyday surfers unexpectedly encountering Slater in line-ups somewhere in the world and finding him friendly and encouraging. Perhaps his humility is one reason for his omission from those lists of the world's greatest sportspeople; perhaps another is surfing's place on the margin, the fact that its relationship with the mainstream remains ambivalent, at best.

But surely the time will come when Slater is a fixture on every sports editor's radar when it comes to the staple of the back pages, the list of greats. He is but one of a handful of surfers to transcend the sport and, in his overwhelming domination of competitive surfing in the modern era, merits comparison with legends from the mainstream of sporting endeavour – the likes of Michael Schumacher, Lance Armstrong and Tiger Woods. Given that his records have been attained despite a three-year hiatus, from 1998 to 2001 during which he didn't even compete, and given also that he continues to surf, aged 40, with the agility of an 18-year-old, it's just possible that Slater eclipses them all.

PART EIGHT

Inspiration

STOKED

There are few things better in life than surfing with dolphins.

Sennen Cove, September, as summer slips into autumn. It's early evening, the sun will soon set over the sea's horizon and, along with six or seven others, I'm enjoying a mellow surf in the amiable, chest high waves which are caressing the beach of this former pilchard fishing station. The water is clear, almost as clear as the sky, for away to the west the humps of the Isles of Scilly can just be discerned. In the foreground, a little offshore from Cape Cornwall – England's only cape, though why this is so I have no idea – lie the Brisons, two islets said to resemble a horizontal Charles de Gaulle, though from my vantage point the reason for this eludes me.

Local surfers use the Brisons as an indicator of swell. If white water can be seen at their base, Sennen Cove will have surf. Sometimes, as on this evening, I find myself in the sea, fully aware of what the waves are like, and yet still drawn to the Brisons. Between waves, I stare at them, marvelling afresh at this part of Cornwall. And just as I look at them, and wonder how far they are from Priest's Cove, which lies next to the Cape, a dolphin breaches just a yard or two from me.

I'm startled. Dolphins in the popular imagination are cute, sociable, perpetually smiling and clever mammals – the closest to the human species you can find in the sea – but in the wild, when one leaps from the water next to you, the cosy cliché is replaced by the intense reality. This is a powerful creature, capable of knocking a surfer unconscious if, by some maritime misjudgement, it breached only to land on man and board.

Of course, dolphins never make such errors. As on this occasion, the dolphin is airborne for an instant and then underwater again, rhythmically surging away to join three or four of its brethren, with just the remnant of salt water spray the closest it comes to hitting me. I turn and scour the sea's surface, as do the other surfers. We're excited by the arrival of the dolphins, the most natural surfers you'll ever find in any ocean; we want to see them again; we don't care how close to us they come. In fact, now that we've got over the dolphins' sudden, unheralded arrival, we want them to get as close as possible. But are we set for disappointment? For some distance away – perhaps 100 yards – the pod breaches again. They seem to be heading out to sea – perhaps to the Brisons.

As we're craning our necks in search of the dolphins, we see a set on the horizon. Within a few seconds the next pulse of oceanic energy will be with us. The better, more experienced, surfers forget all about the dolphins and start paddling for where the waves will peak – the point at which, as they break, they're at their most powerful. We're surfing at a part of the beach known as Black Hut, so called after an octagonal black hut at the foot of the grassy cliff above the sands. I've never seen anyone in it but one surfer I know was once offered the use of it for a summer. What a location – just yards from the mid-part of Whitesand Bay. I guess it's a holiday home, of sorts, now but whatever: a young man has the jump on me, he angles his board as the first wave arrives and jumps to his feet. My wave is next. It's clean and breaking to my left. I take off but, as I look along the face of the wave, I see it again – an explosive burst of grey, blue and silver, angling down the wave, in perfect synchronicity. It's one of the dolphins back to ride a wave, an act that, for humans, serves no purpose other than pleasure. But what does it mean for dolphins? Pleasure, again, is my guess, as I drift down the wave, trimming rather than making any turns, watching the dolphin ahead of me, silently praying that this moment lasts forever.

COLONEL 'MAD JACK' CHURCHILL

The original Bore surfer was anything but boring.

The river does not "swell by degrees, but rolls in with a head . . . foaming and roaring as though it were enraged by the opposition which it encounters". So wrote Thomas Harrel, a local man, in 1824, of the Severn Bore, one of Britain's most spectacular natural phenomena.

In Harrel's wake have come plenty of tales, some apocryphal, some fact. There is talk of dead cows floating upriver, along with fridges, dustbins, empty coffins and other inland flotsam and jetsam. There is talk of whirlpools, of hidden obstacles, of dark, sewage-brown water which is so rank that immersion in it leaves a stench that lasts for days. There is talk of epic rides by Britain's collective of dedicated Bore surfers, of immortalisation in the Guinness Book of Records by the likes of Steve King and David Lawson, of rides that last for miles and of near-death experiences when surfers have mis-timed their exit from the river's fast-flowing current. There is talk – hushed, conspiratorial and yearning – of an inaccessible stretch of the river where the white water mass of the Bore turns into crystalline tubular bliss, and there is the suggestion, to the chagrin of the local surfers who centre their lives around it, that every British surfer should surf the Bore at least once.

There is a lot of talk about the Severn Bore, whose mystery is governed by the moon – as are all the tides on Earth. As the tide from the Atlantic enters the Bristol Channel and continues into the Severn estuary, the huge volume of water funnelled into the narrow channel creates a wave up to 6 ft high. Bores occur year-round, several times a month, but are at their highest around the spring and autumn equinoxes. All the talk about the Bore, of fact or otherwise, means that its peak times see hordes of surfers, and other water users such as canoeists and kayakers, converge and try to ride the murkiest water in Britain.

But for all the talk, for all that the Bore is now a fixture in many surfers' lives, for all the television and video footage, magazine and newspaper articles and chatter on website forums, the man who first surfed the Bore is still its most notable. That man was Colonel 'Mad Jack' Churchill, and his like is rarely seen.

Churchill reputedly owned a Vincent Black Widow motorbike. The Vincent motorbike company's heyday was in the decade following the end of the Second World War, when its Black Lightning model was, for a time, the fastest production motorcycle in the world. In the 1950s, the company also produced the Black Widow, an extraordinary machine that proved to be so deadly that it was eventually outlawed in 37 American states. No wonder: the Black Widow was capable of 200 mph but allied to its incredible capability for speed was its appalling handling. In this, it was similar to other Vincent models, from the Lightning to the Black Shadow and earlier Series Rapide. Large, powerful men tended to be the only riders who could keep a Vincent on the road; of the Black Widow, just a handful – ranging from 10 to 22, depending on who you believe – were made before Vincent ceased trading in 1955.

On 21 July 1955, Churchill set off on his Vincent Black Widow towing something that would have amazed onlookers – a 16 ft surfboard. It was one he had fashioned himself. According to the *Evening Standard*, once he found himself on the banks of the River Severn locals tried to dissuade him from entering the water. "I will be alright," laughed Churchill, who then – in the same year that Russell Wright set the motorbike world land-speed record of 184 mph on a Vincent HRD in New Zealand – made history in becoming the first person to surf the Severn Bore.

Churchill rode the Bore for a mile and a half, having learnt to surf in Australia. Remarkable though it was, the feat was far from Churchill's most notable exploit. He was a professional soldier whose courage saw him awarded the Distinguished Service Order twice and the Military Cross, and whose eccentricity was arguably just as impressive. Churchill – also known as 'Fighting Jack' – once said that "any officer who goes into action without his sword is improperly armed", and he fought throughout the Second World War with a longbow, arrows and a Scottish broadsword. On 27 May 1940 at L'Epinette near Bethune, Churchill became the only man to shoot dead an enemy soldier with an arrow loosed from a longbow.

Born in Surrey in 1906, Churchill joined the army in 1926. He served in South East Asia and having completed a signals course at Poona, decided to ride a Zenith motorcycle 1,500 miles across India. In Burma, Churchill had to traverse railway bridges with the Zenith by stepping on sleepers (between which was often a dramatic drop) and pushing the bike along the rails; his odyssey also saw him crash into a water buffalo. No surprise, perhaps, that Churchill found life boring when his regiment returned to Britain. He retired from the army after 10 years' service, only to re-enlist in 1939. His conduct in the Second World War might easily have been the creation of an especially imaginative *Boy's Own* writer, entailing Commando raids in Norway and Italy, leading a landing force ashore while playing the bagpipes (at which he excelled), tunnelling out of a prison at Sachsenhausen Camp, near Berlin and commanding the 5th (Scottish) Parachute Battalion, thereby becoming the only officer to command both a Commando and a Parachute battalion. It was, though, all true.

If Churchill's courage became the stuff of legend, earning him his 'Mad' and 'Fighting' Jack monikers, his sense of fair play was equally well-developed. "You have treated us well," he wrote to the German commander whose forces had captured him after a raid on the island of Brac. "If, after the war, you are ever in England and Scotland, come and have dinner with my wife and myself." The note later saved the life of Captain Hans Thornerr when the Yugoslavs sought to execute him as a war criminal.

Churchill may well have been serious when he bemoaned the end of the war to a friend: "You know, if it hadn't been for those damned Yanks we could have kept the war going for another 10 years." Before the term 'adrenalin junkie' had been invented he was its blueprint, and yet he was a man with a sensitive side too, a student of history and poetry who was known for his compassion to animals (even including insects). After the war, he served in Jerusalem before returning to Britain where he was second-in-command of the Army Apprentices School at Chepstow. There then came a two-year stint as Chief Instructor at the Land/Air Warfare School in Australia – where Churchill, by then middle-aged, threw his abundant energy into learning to surf.

Churchill's Severn Bore ride was witnessed by a local farmer and his son. Little could any of the trio know what would become of Bore riding, that it would become a way of life for surfers not just in Britain, but in a number of other countries too.

As for Mad Jack, after his retirement from the army in 1959 he busied himself with his hobby of buying and refurbishing steamboats on the Thames. He also made radio-controlled model boats but was unable to live without at least something in the way of excitement. He continued to take part in motorbike speed trials and occasionally enjoyed baffling commuters on his journey home by hurling his attaché case out of a train window. It would land in his back garden, and he wouldn't have to carry it home.

What became of Churchill's Black Widow is not known. But like the man himself, were it to emerge today it would surely be priceless.

OMG (TAKE 2)

Come hell or high water, Mark Cunningham might just be the best waverider in the world.

Forget conventional surfing for a minute. Forget it for half an hour, or for as long as it takes to read this story. Forget Laird Hamilton's millennium wave at Teahupoo – that which *Surfer* magazine trailed with a simple, perfect 'oh my god'. Forget even the insane waves caught by Dylan Longbottom, Laurie Turner, Bruce Irons, Nathan Fletcher and others, when they decided to ignore the Tahitian government's Code Red advisory and tow-surf massive, life-threatening Teahupoo on 27 August 2011.

Forget all this, amazing as it is, for in the form of veteran North Shore lifeguard Mark Cunningham, there is a man who is as comfortable in the ocean as a dolphin. He, too, has ridden the waves of Teahupoo, but unlike Hamilton, Longbottom, Irons *et al*, he didn't use a jetski. He didn't use a surfboard. He didn't even use a bodyboard. All he used was a pair of fins. The resulting rides, by a man who is as humble as he is extraordinary, are among the most beautiful ever witnessed.

They were caught on camera in *Come Hell or High Water*, a 2011 film by American surfer Keith Malloy. The film celebrates the art of bodysurfing – the purest form of surfing there is. To watch it is for the irreligious and agnostic alike to wonder if there is a God, after all – and if there is, whether what he created in Cunningham is the representative of the divine on earth.

Malloy himself hails from Ventura County, California, where he grew up on a ranch 15 miles from the beach. Tall, sporting a fulsome beard and in his habitual garb of checked shirt and brown trousers, Malloy, who was born in 1974, looks more frontiersman of the American Dream than surf dude. But his surfing credentials are as good as they get. He began surfing before he was six and went on to qualify for the World Championship Tour. Appearances in cult surf films such as *Thicker Than Water, Waveriders* and *Step Into Liquid* helped consolidate a persona that blends thoughtfulness with action in a way rarely seen in the surfing world. It is, however, also apparent in his brothers, Chris and Dan. Chris is a renowned big wave surfer who has been invited to compete in the Eddie Aikau Invitational; Dan finished second in the US Open 2000 but thereafter gave up the contest scene in favour of intrepid travel (and a brief stint as a model on Ralph Lauren's books).

The Malloy brothers are widely respected in surfing, not least as environmentalists. They are all ambassadors for Patagonia, the outdoor clothing brand with a conscience, set up by Yves Chouinard in 1972. They also help design ecologically sound wetsuits, apparel and accessories and each drives a car powered by vegetable oil. But if the very title of Chouinard's second book, an account of his business life called *Let My People Go Surfing*, might be enough to give hope to surfers ensnared in corporate machines the world over, Keith Malloy's star bodysurfer in *Come Hell or High Water* would surely make them resign in search of the lives they crave.

"It just seemed so real and genuine," says Cunningham of bodysurfing, in a voiceover of footage showing him hurtling along the faces of waves at good-sized Pipeline in 1979. "So pure and so simple, as tight with nature as I could possibly get."

Cunningham, who grew up in the Niu Valley on the east side of Oahu and learnt to bodysurf at Sandy Beach, is so mesmerizingly good at bodysurfing that he seems not merely tight with nature but a vital, constituent element of the waves he rides. And while many surfers talk of 'conquering' waves, 'gouging' turns and generally ripping and shredding, Cunningham's lexicon is one of humility. "Hawaii has shown me that it's not always about the biggest wave or the best barrel. It's just about being in the ocean and having fun."

From 1976, when the tall, gangly Cunningham became a Hawaii lifeguard, to the early 1990s, he had more fun than just about anyone at Oahu's best bodysurfing spots, dominating bodysurfing competitions and line-ups from Makapuu and Sandy Beach to Pipeline and Point Panic. The latter, a break on the South Shore, was always a favourite of Cunningham's, and Malloy's film reveals a crew of chiefly indigenous Hawaiians revelling in the fast, hollow waves served up in summer by this Honolulu jewel. But anyone who thinks that bodysurfing is just catching a wave and straight-lining into the sand should think again. Cunningham, and the Honolulu crew, catch waves effortlessly, turn and trim – one arm outstretched, the other trailing – for as long as they like, getting barrelled, riding on their backs and twisting with the suppleness of gymnasts along the way.

That this is all about play is neatly distilled in a scene in which three men, evidently on a ranch à la that on which Malloy grew up, make a small ramp in a dusty yard, then try to pilot a remote control car up and over it. What seems to be an attempt to refashion the ramp results in the creation of a small, rectangular piece of wood, but the film soon switches to a tropical backdrop where a sumptuous head high left-hander is peeling over a reef. A bodysurfer proceeds to catch wave after wave, planing along the surface using the piece of wood held out in front of him by both arms.

The inspiration for the film came from Cunningham. "I got the idea for the movie about 10 years ago," says Malloy. "It was then that I started hanging out with Mark, bodysurfing every day in Hawaii. My brothers and I enjoyed his company and we learned a lot from him, not just about bodysurfing but about the ocean."

One session with Cunningham at Pipeline is etched on Malloy's mind. "The waves were only about head high but it was a full moon, so we stayed out after sunset for about two hours. The power had gone out so there were no houselights on the beach. I think bodysurfing by moonlight enabled us to see the waves even better. The sandbar was perfect and we were getting these little peelers for about 30-50 yards. It was surreal and happened on 3 February about 10 years ago. I remember because it was my sister Mary's birthday and I'll never forget that."

The genesis for *Come Hell or High Water* came, then, from bodysurfing with Cunningham at the turn of the millennium – around the same time as Laird Hamilton's OMG wave at Teahupoo. "Back then we started talking about making a film," confirms Malloy. "I knew the underwater imagery would be beautiful and it'd be such a unique way to see this sport. Bodysurfing takes place 80 per cent under the water, so to me filming a bodysurfer underwater would be the only real way to show what's happening when you're riding the waves."

Hence, then, the ravishing cinematography in *Come Hell or High Water,* for which Scott Soens won a *Surfer* magazine award. But there was another prompt for Malloy. "Another big reason I wanted to make the film was that the bodysurfers themselves are such great characters. I knew they would be fantastic subjects to interview and film and follow. Bodysurfing attracts such an inclusive and yet varied group. There are judges, trashmen, doctors and landscapers – they're all out there in the ocean, having a blast."

And, when they appear in the form of Thomas VanMelum, they are also very large. But VanMelum's bulk – he looks more like a weightlifter than a surfer – might just be perfect for the bodysurfing break with which he is synonymous: The Wedge, at the east end of the Balboa Peninsula in Newport Beach, California. This highly dangerous, bone-shattering wave attracts a collective of bodysurfers for whom the adjective 'characterful' is a magnificent understatement. Malloy gives them due respect in his film, but lets them speak for themselves rather than engage in undue reverence. No surprise given the looping, looming, ludicrous peaks at The Wedge, that one bodysurfer says simply "We should all be dead", while even the intimidating and muscular, not to mention moustachioed and pipe-smoking, VanMelum reveals that one wave caused him to bite off the end of his tongue.

But it is Cunningham's world that is the centrepiece of *Come Hell or High Water.* Even a scene of bodysurfing a river in Montana can't steal the show – although a delicately handled vignette of a father taking his autistic son bodysurfing, and delighting in his pure, abandoned joy, comes close. But Cunningham is the master, and in Teahupoo, Cunningham's world emerges as nothing short of art.

"Teahupoo was one of the most incredible bodysurfing experiences I've ever had," says Malloy. "We had the perfect size swell and the best bodysurfers in the world. We were so lucky because everything just came together. I spent quite a bit of time behind the camera, but also got to bodysurf myself. I had some of the best rides of my life. The water is crystal clear there, you can see the reef below and you're riding one of the most powerful waves in the world. It was just an amazing feeling."

Malloy and Cunningham took a boat out to the notorious reef at Teahupoo. Cunningham, experienced as he is, was not free of nerves. "People had been telling me for years that you could bodysurf Teahupoo," he says, "but even with years and years of experience at Pipeline I was really anxious about it."

But in the event, Cunningham – who lifeguarded for 18 years at Pipeline – glides into the big, barrelling, glistening and crystalline waves of Teahupoo as if he had been bodysurfing them all his life. The sequence in the film makes for its climax, and is accompanied by 'I Am The Buffalo' by The Phoenix Foundation. It's a rapturous, melodic counterpoint to Cunningham's epiphany as a teenager as he sat on a beach, watching the sea, and thinking of a bodysurfing session he had just had. "This is as clear and beautiful and meaningful to me as anything in the world," he thought. "If it's giving me pleasure, if it's making me happy, why shouldn't I continue to do this as long as I can?"

Come hell or high water, it's a safe bet that that's exactly what Mark Cunningham will do for the rest of his life. He may not be as fêted as Hamilton, and his Teahupoo session may not have been when a Code Red warning was in place, but to watch Cunningham bodysurf is to marvel, while to encounter his modesty and intelligence is to utter a quiet OMG – and, if you're stuck in a job that keeps you from the ocean, to make plans to change your life.

DR SARAH AND THE MEANING OF SURFING

Could it be that surfing is at its most amazing when it's at its simplest?

This isn't a tale of big waves or epic rides. No one dies in this story; no one nearly dies either. It's not about getting shacked in a 10-second barrel and it doesn't involve smashing any lips. There's not a radical move in sight and if you're looking for a backside 360 degree air reverse, look elsewhere. This is just a story about two people going for a surf.

This particular surf happened in the summer, in the far west of Cornwall. It was a balmy, still and beautiful day. I'd been writing for much of it, happy enough to devote myself to whatever deadline it was in the knowledge that there wasn't much by way of surf. A late lunchtime walk with the dogs had further vindicated this decision; at low tide, the whole of Sennen Cove – mainland Britain's most westerly beach – was unruffled by either swell or wind. There wasn't a wave to be seen, just the thinnest wisps of white water caressing the sand. It was a perfect day for tourists, for swimmers, for families with their children. They were making the most of it, frolicking on the sand and in the sea, splashing around, running back and forth, building sandcastles and eating ice-creams under the clear, crisp light. I returned home, to my deadline.

In the evening, around 6pm, with my deadline met, something prompted me to load up my car with my board and go back for a surf check. In the car park above a beach known as Spot G, I gazed toward the horizon. While earlier the outline of the Isles of Scilly had been clearly visible, now a diffuse haze hung in the air merging sea and sky in a deliquescent blue-grey. Closer to shore, I could see four or five basking sharks, benign creatures drawn to this part of Cornwall in a summer search for plankton. They're benign, but big; their large frames and prominent dorsal fins dominated the middle-ground, momentarily distracting me from realizing that below me the left-hander at Spot G was producing immaculate, irresistible and unridden shoulder-high waves.

The high tide push sometimes does this at Spot G. It can be flat everywhere else and yet the tidal surge creates surfable waves. But as I looked on, I realized that what I was seeing was more than merely the workings of the tide. I was witnessing the first pulse of a new swell.

There are over 500 steps from the car park at Spot G to its beach. I made it down them in record time. I couldn't believe that no one else was there. Locals know that Spot G can have a wave on even the quietest of days; moreover, it was summer, the silly season, the time when basking sharks get mistaken for Great Whites by Britain's tabloid press and when the chances are that the line-up will include every would-be surfer in the land – how could I be so lucky as to be about to surf the place on my own?

I wasn't. As I stood up from tying my leash and took my first steps into the sea, I saw a woman paddling out. She had another 20 yards to go and then she'd be there, on the peak, ready to ride one of the glassy, perfect lefts. I fancied I recognised her, but wasn't sure. I started paddling out; as I did so, the woman caught a wave. She glided smoothly along its sensual face, trimming in the pocket rather than turning, and as she sped down the line I recognized the blonde dreadlocks and tanned face – it was Dr Sarah.

Upon reaching the peak I turned to look back to the shore. Dr Sarah had ridden her wave all the way to the beach, and had just begun to paddle back to the line-up. Just then, a set wave came my way, a glorious, peeling left that enabled a series of smooth carves and cutbacks, the pleasure of which was, it seemed to me, a gift from God. I rode the wave the 100 yards or so all the way to the sand.

Dr Sarah and I continued with this routine for so many waves that we lost count of them. A couple of times, we were in the line-up at the same time. We don't know each other well; we're just two of the local surfers in this part of the world. Indeed, if we've seen each other in the sea more times than either of us would care to remember, we've only ever met once on land (we were shopping in Tesco). I call Sarah 'Dr Sarah' because I'm reliably informed that she is a doctor, but where she practises, or whether she's a specialist, or a surgeon, or whatever, I have no idea. I know also that Sarah plays in a much-loved west Cornwall band called Pond Life, and I think she plays the sax. Again though, I'm not sure. The fact is that Dr Sarah and I barely know each other.

We didn't say much that time at Spot G, but we did agree that we couldn't believe our luck. How blessed we were to have a flawless left-hander to ourselves at a break that would normally be overrun? And what a break, too. Spot G is backed by granite cliffs, its water is crystal clear, dolphins and seals are regulars in the line-up and the ambience is other-worldly and ancient. That summer evening, the basking sharks continued to drift some 100 yards beyond the line-up, while a handful of children swam in the shallows. As the sun began to set, with the pulse of tide and swell filling up the white sands of the beach, the opaque horizon was tinged first with pink, then with an almost livid bright green-to-blue, and all the while Dr Sarah and I remained the only surfers in the sea.

When we met the next time in the supermarket, (I was looking for a tin of tomatoes; Sarah was on the same quest) we talked about that session at Spot G. By then two or three years had passed, and yet we both remembered it with complete clarity, and we both agreed that it was the best surf either of us had ever had.

I can think of no other pursuit that can create such an extraordinary shared experience between two people who barely know each other. Only surfing can do this. Only surfing can provide so blissful and ineffable a sense of peace, of oneness with nature and one's fellow human beings. Air reverses, intense barrels and 40 ft waves are optional; to be stoked – to fall in love with the ocean and what it can yield – all you need to do is ride a wave.

ACKNOWLEDGEMENTS

The reprint of this book retains all of its previous acknowledgements, but I've updated a couple of things. Huge thanks go to:

- Jeremy Atkins and the team at Fernhurst Books. Quite simply, they've done a brilliant job.
- Everyone who helped me put this book together. A number of busy professional surfers and others involved in the surf world made time to tell me their tales: you'll be somewhere in the book and when you see your name it comes with much gratitude. Special thanks for extra help must go to Pam Chater, Alex Williams, Al Mackinnon, Gabe Davies, Cassandra Murnieks, Tony Butt, Victoria Gaertig, Caroline Davidson, Vince Medeiros, Chris Nelson, Greg Martin, Tony Plant, Tup and Stef, and Tom and Ernie at Finisterre.
- Gwynedd Haslock, whose Sea and Surf Reflections (Mid Cornwall Publishing, 2010) is as inspirational as the lady herself.
- Robert Barr Smith, for his excellent research into the life of Colonel 'Mad Jack' Churchill (see www.wwiihistorymagazine.com), and Brad Melekian, whose piece on Andy Irons (see www.outside.online.com) was ground-breaking.
- Mark Tyers, for the one that got away.
- Matt Warshaw: as ever, his Encyclopaedia of Surfing is the source of all surfing wisdom (and a lot of cast-iron factual info).

- The man in the east himself, Neil Watson – a wonderful, constant an sterling help throughout the writing. Sadly, Neil passed away on 3 December 2014. I was honoured to write his obituary for The Times – see https://www.thetimes.co.uk/article/neil-watson-g9xj88ftrt3. I know he's much missed by his son Dan and daughter Justine, as well as the East Anglian surfing community and beyond.

Talking of Neil, he and I would often discuss a book I began to write, in 2014, called Winter's Tale. This was to be the story of Russell Winter, the man who is by far and away the most successful British surfer to date. Russ contacted me and asked if I'd be interested in writing his life story; it took me all of a millisecond to say 'yes'. People checking out this book will realise my interest stemmed not just from admiration for what Russ achieved as a British surfer, but because, as recounted in Do You Know Russell Winter?, he is notoriously media shy. I'd had several near-miss interviews with Russ over the years: now, at last, he wanted to tell his story. There was no way I wasn't going to write this one.

Russ and I met on many occasions in Newquay. I took notes, read old surf mags, did a heap of research and talked to his parents, Mick and Anita. I wrote the opening few chapters and talked to plenty of UK and international surfers. Kelly Slater and Martin Potter gave me a few lines, Potter with a smile on his face, Slater deadpan, inscrutable, impenetrable. The consensus was consistent. If you know Russ, you'll know he's one hell of a surfer – and one hell of a hellraiser too.

A year or so into the writing, Russ decided to put the book on hold. Another year or two later, and my life had gone in a different direction too – I'd become a dad again and gone back into the law. I now spend most of my time reviewing manuscripts and film scripts for legal issues. I'm not sure I'd have the time to write Winter's Tale if Russ picked up the phone and said we're on again.

But my own eventful life tells me that without writing, things aren't right. So, Russ, if you read this: I hope all is well. One day we'll finish Winter's Tale.

I can only close by paying tribute to the two amazing women in my life – my partner Caroline and our daughter Maud. Some things are way, way more important than surfing

Other titles you might be interested in...

Our *ULTIMATE* Series

Collections of 100 extraordinary experiences illustrated with striking full page photography

The other titles in our *AMAZING* Series

All available from **www.fernhurstbooks.com**

Visit our website to discover our full range of titles and all that we have to offer. Here you can also register to receive news, details of new books and exclusive special offers.